THE VITAL LINK

MW01258672

INTERCESSORY PRAYER

Dear Marie,

I pray that God's richest blessings upon your life!

Dr. Sun Fannin   5/14/22

DR. SUN FANNIN

Printed in the United States of America

First Printing, 2022

ISBN: 978-1-947939-97-4

ENDORSEMENTS

"This book on intercession will be a necessary study for all who desire to know, experience and walk with Jesus in a greater measure!"

– Dr. Sherill Piscopo
Senior Pastor, Evangel Christian Churches, Roseville, MI
Author, *Spiritual Warfare A Manual For Inner Healing & Deliverance*

"Now is the time for us all to receive a fresh impartation of the Spirit of Intercession, and this book will be invaluable!"

– Dr. David Cannistraci
Senior Pastor, Gateway City Church,
San Jose California Author, *Apostles and the Emerging Apostolic Movement* and *Let's Talk About Teams*

"Get ready to dig deep and go deep. This book will challenge your prayer walk and your gift as an intercessor in ways you never thought possible!"

– Drs. Simon and Trish Presland
Co-founders, God's Pathways Co-founders,
Aim Higher Professional Life Coach Certification

ACKNOWLEDGMENTS

Rev. Rachel Lee and Rev. Jael Roh, for spending countless hours translating my book from Korean to English. I am so thankful for you are my spiritual granddaughters! You both have grown to be beautiful women of God, and you are my pride and Joy.

Dr. Sherill Piscopo, your help and encouragement, and proofreading skills—and for the beautiful foreword! You are the best spiritual mom and pastor anyone could ever ask for. I appreciate you for countless time you have given me, for the wise counsel, and for guiding me to be a better leader to carry the gospel for the Christ.

Dr. David Cannistraci, thank you for your foreword! You have always shown God's love and acceptance towards me. You are far more than just my friend; you are my spiritual leader and pastor as well. You are an encourager and true example of Christ.

My son, Pastor Jody Ballenger, for all your help in putting this book together. You are such a loving and faithful son, and a courageous leader in the Body of Christ. Thank you for your years of supporting me, especially during the Sunshine Ministries yearly conference. You always work hard and want to serve God with excellency. I love and appreciate you more than you ever know!

Dr. Simon, for worked many months to organize, edit, and help complete this book. Your patient is absolutely beyond what I could express. Your excellency and perfectionism to do what is right gives me all confidence to trust your work. I trust you to take care of all my books, including a new one coming in the future.

Last but not least, I want to thank my heavenly Father, who has always faithfully guided me to fulfill His calling and vision for me. God never fails to fulfill His promises. He always watches over me to stir and motivate me to follow His will and plans. I give all my honor and glory to my Jesus forever more.

DEDICATION

I dedicate this book to my late husband, Pastor Larry Fannin, for 41 years of marriage and 37 years of ministry. You believed in my gifts and calling, and always supported me unconditionally. You gave me constant encouragement to reach my full potential in Christ. You encouraged me to believe that if God gave me a vision or a dream, I could not allow anything or anyone to stop me from following His plan. You were my mentor, teacher, pastor, lover, big brother, and best friend.

To my spiritual father, the late bishop Dr. Jerry Piscopo. You were the only true father I ever had. You believed in my calling as an "overseas" apostle, and sent me to Asia as a representative of EACM. You trusted God's calling on my life, and you mentored me and guided me to fulfill my destiny. Most of my inner healing and deliverance ministry was guided by you. I thank you for your impartation and the unconditional love you poured into my life.

FOREWORD

Dr. Sherill Piscopo

Intercession has always been an intriguing aspect of prayer that I was drawn to. My heart yearned to know Jesus in a deeper way. No matter how much I read and studied, I knew in my heart there was more. Then, God brought Sun Fannin into our lives. I read her book, *If My People*. I knew just from reading, that this woman not only knew how to fast and pray, but demonstrated in her life a relationship with God that I desired and needed. I contacted her and she prayed before accepting my invitation to come and share at Evangel. I had never experienced that with a speaker. It has always been our belief that you invite speakers that will leave an impartation on you and your people, not just someone to come and motivate, receive an offering and move on. I was awed that God was inquired of and we had both heard Him say, "Come." She had interceded, fasted and inquired of God about Bishop and I and Evangel. It was an encouragement that this was an assignment not just another "speaking engagement."

The remainder of the story is history. She and her late husband, Dr. Larry Fannin and Evangel Christian Church Greenfield, Indiana are family to us. This woman has travelled the world sharing what God is saying especially about prayer, fasting, inner healing, deliverance and intercession. Our ministry has always been one of restoration, inner healing and deliverance. God has knit us together for such a time as this! Religion is man's attempt to touch God, but prayer, intercession, inner healing and deliverance is God's way of reaching man. The result is a changed life that causes us to intercede for others so that they too will experience this incredible God.

This book on intercession will be a necessary study for all who desire to know, experience and walk with Jesus in a greater measure. Dr. Sun Fannin has written a treatise that will take you into another level in prayer, but also through her life experience cause you to yearn for a deeper walk in your own relationship with Jesus as you maneuver through this life's journey.

Dr. Sun makes it plain so that the reader can obtain that same connection with the Lord in their prayer life. Because we live in a time like no other, this refreshing, hope and impartation is a necessity. You need to meet the Holy Spirit and be filled with His power to pick up where Jesus left off in the earth. As you seek Him in intercession, you find that you are able to lay your life down for another to become His hands and feet.

This is not just another book on prayer. This book will give you training, experience and a revelation of the Holy Spirit to impact you in a new way. You can encounter Him and observe how He can use you to reach a lost world and leave an indelible imprint for God's Kingdom.

It is my prayer and wish for you to ingest this book and make it a part of your daily walk with God. This is a time for the saints to arise. The next great move of God will be through relationship, prayer and intercession as God moves through everyday people like you and me! Read, feast and enjoy!

Dr. Sherill Piscopo
Senior Pastor, Evangel Christian Churches, Roseville, MI
Author, *Spiritual Warfare A Manual For Inner Healing & Deliverance*

FOREWORD

Dr. David Cannistraci

Like other leaders of my generation, intercession has been a lifelong passion of mine. Many of us grew up spiritually in an era when God was doing new things in prayer. What is now called the worldwide prayer movement had its beginnings in those years. Like many, I watched in awe as God released the anointing of prayer and intercession across the globe in churches, networks, stadiums and conferences. Because it was so life-giving, I read and watched everything I could about prayer, intercession and spiritual warfare. I studied the examples of great men and women of prayer, both contemporary and historic. As a result, nothing has marked my life and ministry more deeply than the worldwide prayer movement.

The worldwide prayer movement has also shaped my life by connecting me with great leaders. For more than 40 years as a pastor, author and speaker, I've had the privilege of knowing and working with leading voices in the prayer movement like Dr. C. Peter Wagner, Cindy Jacobs, Dutch Sheets, John Benefiel and John Dawson. I've also connected with many others who were less well-known, but also knew what they were doing when it came to prayer and intercession.

One such leader is Dr. Sun Fannin. Kathy and I met Sun over three decades ago through the late Dr. Jerry Piscopo, and his wife, Dr. Sherill Piscopo, who have been like family to us. When they introduced us to Sun, it was love at first sight. Sun had the same passion for prayer that we had—though her story was very different from ours. As we welcomed her ministry into our church, we grew to appreciate her even more. Sun and her late husband Larry have been lifelong friends ever since.

I can't think of anyone I'd rather hear from on the subject of intercession than Sun Fannin. Sun has written and taught on intercession around the world, but more importantly, she lives and imparts what she knows. Kathy and I have been in her home, and she has been in ours. Sun has the right character and lifestyle. She has a pure heart and a solid grasp of the Scriptures. And she expresses her message of prayer with refreshing simplicity, honesty and clarity.

Intercessory Prayer: The Vital Link Between Heaven and Earth is an important book for several reasons. First, it unpacks intercession in Sun's trademark manner: it is clear, Biblical, inspirational and accessible. Others have written on intercession from theological and mystical perspectives. Sun Fannin offers us a needed practical guide into the ministry of intercession.

This book is also important because of its incredible timing. After some of the most tumultuous years many of us have ever experienced, prayer and intercession will be a key source of spiritual renewal and even resurrection for many. Now is the time for us all to receive a fresh impartation of the Spirit of Intercession, and this book will be invaluable in that regard.

I am grateful for the remarkable gift that my dear friend Dr. Sun Fannin has given to us in these pages. I pray that your copy of this book will become well-worn and carefully followed as you take your place in the next chapter of this worldwide movement of prayer.

Dr. David Cannistraci
Senior Pastor, Gateway City Church, San Jose California
Author, *Apostles and the Emerging Apostolic Movement* and
Let's Talk About Teams

PREFACE

I thank God for His blessing and grace to be able to write a book about intercession. He taught me and blessed me so much throughout the years, and this book contains a portion of what I've learned and experienced. I feel overwhelmed with the responsibility for what this book contains, and how it can change lives. However, God's word is true: "… My grace is sufficient for you, for my power is made perfect in weakness. Therefore I will boast all the more gladly about my weaknesses, so that Christ's power may rest on me" (2 Corinthians 12:9, NIV).

I can write only what I've experienced in my walk with God, however, some people may not agree with my personal experiences. I pray that you will overlook any differences, and see the many breakthroughs that I've witnessed through having a deep intercessory prayer life. I'm asking God to challenge you to go to a deeper level on prayer, and to "stir up the gift that is within you" (2 Timothy 1:6). I exhort you to pray and intercede for your nation, loved ones, the Body of Christ, and for the unsaved like never before!

I have not yet "arrived" with regards to intercessory prayer. I am far from perfect and have much more to learn. But one thing I can say for sure is that I am open to hear and learn from God, as long as I live.

I was preaching and teaching about intercessory prayer before I ever realized that I was called as intercessor. My heart has been burdened to tell people about prayer, ever since I received Jesus as my Lord and Savior in January, 1976.

Over the years, I have watched God answer my prayers, but not always according to what I wanted or the way I expected; but God knew my situations better, and gave me the answers I desperately needed. The results were always amazing and helped me to grow in God, and to trust Him more with my life. My soul has prospered, and my life has been so blessed beyond my understanding. Ever since my salvation, God has given me so much energy and excitement to help and encourage others to pray and intercede, so they, too, can experience the same power of God—He is the same yesterday, today, and forever!

God is looking for committed intercessors to pray and intercede effectively to move His hand. For us to see the move of God in our prayer life, we must have a clean heart. Therefore, we cannot allow darkness, such as hurts and wounds, to creep in and hinder our prayers.

God doesn't want us to hold onto hurt, which is why He taught us how to forgive. If there's a root of unforgiveness within us, we can never stand in the gap and fulfill the calling of a mediator. God has made it clear that forgiveness is not an option, it's a requirement (Matt. 6:14-16). Forgiving our enemies is an opportunity for us to pull out the whole root of the Devil's work. But it is extremely difficult for us to forgive with our own strength. However, it is impossible to love our enemy, show kindness to them, and bless them with our own human strength (Luke 6:27-28). There is only one way to love our enemy, show kindness and to bless them. Therefore, we must seek God as to how this person harmed us and what led them to do so. In that moment of hurt, we invite Jesus into that situation, so that we can receive inner healing. Only then true forgiveness is possible.

First, we have to see the problem within us and realize and understand where this scar came from. This can give us compassion for our enemy and we intercede for them. Hating someone is like inviting the Devil into our lives. We are allowing him to bind us, and he will destroy us first before he destroys our offender. We must refuse the Devil enterance into our mind. Once the Devil has an open door into our lives, the forces of evil will dominate our hearts and slowly extinguish the work of the Holy Spirit, and the inspiration of the Holy Spirit can't manifest. Therefore, we cannot pray according to God's will and live in His will, which can eventually destroy us.

Permitting the realm of darkness within us means that we are opening the door for evil spirits to work in that realm. Intercessors must learn the method of defeating the Devil. The Devil has been successful in deceiving mankind for thousands of years; hence he knows how to deceive us very well. People tend to believe the Devil's lies more than God's Word. Intercessors must not agree with these lies, such as the whispers that we can't do all things through Christ who gives us strength (Philippians 4:13).

Spiritual battle and spiritual breakthrough are inseparable. Those who want spiritual breakthrough *must* go through spiritual battle. In order to have victory, there is a definite price to pay. What intercessors must remember is that whenever we go through a new door of ministry, we must prepare for a new spiritual battle. Our adversary is always ready to attack us with all kinds of methods and tactics to stop us from starting a new work of God. The Devil doesn't want us to take back the territory, family, and ministry that he's stolen, and he will resist us from setting foot in any new territory. What we must also remember is when we are experiencing an intense spiritual battle, then we can expect even a greater spiritual breakthrough. The greater the war, the greater the victory!

I am forever grateful for knowing Jesus as my Lord and Savior. I couldn't imagine living my life without my Lord Jesus, who is everything to me. I give all glory and honor to my Lord and Savior!

Dr. Sun Fannin
Founder, Sunshine International Ministries,
Co-founder, Evangel Church,
Greenfield, Indiana

INTRODUCTION

About four years ago, God laid on my heart to write this intercessory prayer book. I have already written several books but not on
intercession. I had no idea how to write this book or what God wanted
to include. So I spent several days in prayer, inquiring of the Lord for His
guidance and direction.

When I was working on my last book *Inner Healing and Restoration*,
God showed me that I would have at least ten published books before He
took me home. At the time, I had written five books, and I was excited to
start this one but also felt apprehensive.

One day, I felt the Lord was guiding me to gather up all my notes
that I preached for years at churches, seminars, and conferences. Surprisingly, I found many intercessory prayer teaching notes! I knew then that
with my own intercessory breakthrough experiences, I had what I needed
to start writing.

When God gives me a vision, one that I know is absolutely from
him, there is nothing that can stop me from fulfilling it. Night and day,
I began to write, whenever I had any extra time. I had a clear vision for
the purpose of my writing, and I had good motivation as well. The more
I wrote, the more the excitement increased.

Then I hit an almost insurmountable event in my life.

My late husband, Pastor Larry, had been sick for a long time, but
his sickness was getting worse and his body began to deteriorate. He
needed my full attention, and I couldn't stretch myself to continue writing. Eventually I stopped and put my notes away for almost three years.
Sadly, my husband passed on June 20th, 2021.

A few months prior to my husband's death, I got up early one morning, and felt God urging me to finish my intercessory prayer book.

For the next three months, I took care of my husband during the day, and worked on my book while he slept at night. It was so much easier to write in Korean, and my spiritual daughters then translated my writing into English. They did an excellent job and I am so proud of them.

After my husband passed, I was going through a very difficult time, and I could hardly do anything but cry. I asked God to give me 30 days to mourn, like Israel mourned 30 days for Moses's death.

On the 30th day, I was in bed praying, I heard God speak to my heart. I got up in hurry and I wrote down everything He spoke to my heart.

1. Fix your eyes on Jesus (Heb. 12:2)
2. Be strong (Deut. 31:6) (Ps.23:4) (Isa. 41:10)
3. Think positive (Phil. 4:8)
4. Have a heavenly mind (Rev. 21:4) (John 14:1-2)
5. Focus on your vision and dream (Pro. 29:18) (Ps. 27:4)

After I received this encouraging message from the Lord, I made a little card with these five points and posted it on the shower door so I could see it every morning and memorize what God had told me. Every time I felt lost and lonely, and was going through hard times, I kept reminding myself of His message. Soon after, I had the strength to focus on God's vision for this book, and I began to write again.

God was faithful to guide me every step, and the vision He gave me for this book is now fulfilled. He provided the finances for editing and publication, and I received two forewords from the people I honor the most in my life. How blessed I am!

When God urged me to get to start writing again, I also felt His burden for intercession on behalf of our nation, and His body, the Church. The book you hold in your hands is the result of the vision God gave me and the burden I felt. God's word is true: "I can do all things through Christ who strengthens me." (Phil. 4:13, NKJV).

As you read this book, my prayer is that you will be stirred in your spirit to pray and intercede for your loved ones, family, church, city, and nation.

Join me with your intercession. Let's fill the gap. Let's build a hedge of protection around the broken souls, families, churches, cities, and nations.

God's richest blessings upon your life!

Dr. Sun Fannin

CHAPTER 1

GOD IS SEARCHING
FOR AN INTERCESSOR

Called as an Intercessor

My late husband, Pastor Larry, and I planted a church in Greenfield, Indiana in 1981. For 37 years we were senior pastors, while my son, Jody, was an associate pastor. In 2018, we stepped down and now support Pastor Jody and his wife, Eunjoo, who are the current senior pastors.

I founded Sunshine International Ministries in 1985 and began to travel all over the United States, sharing God's Word and my testimony. As God continually poured His grace upon me, my ministry has spread worldwide and is known among other nations. At the beginning of my ministry, people started calling me *Evangelist* Sun Fannin everywhere I went. Then, people began to call me *Pastor* or *Teacher* Sun Fannin. Soon after, people began to refer to me as *Intercessor* Sun Fannin. Just when I thought this was it, people began to refer to me as a *prophetess* and *apostle*, as well as a *mentor* or *spiritual mother*.

From the very beginning of Sunshine International Ministries until now, I have traveled to several countries and ministered to multitudes. However, I am here today because God gradually expanded and developed my ministry before I even recognized or realized it. Ephesians

4:11-12 talks about the five-fold ministries (apostle, prophet, evangelist, pastor, and teacher). Anyone that experiences these five-fold ministries today may think of how awesome these roles are, but if someone were to ask me who I am today, I would say that I am *Intercessor* Sun Fannin.

A Beautiful Calling

It is my conviction that I believe being recognized as an *intercessor* and being called as a *mediator* before God is more beautiful than any other special title or function. I am certain that being an intercessor is the most important calling and mission that God has given me, even though other missions are as important as well. I believe in my heart that if intercessory prayer is missing in our lives, we will have difficulties enduring any ministry position or responsibility God puts us in. We need to be intercessors *first* who are willing to sacrifice and pray for others, then we can properly administer the five-fold ministry gifts that God desires.

I first understood that God had called me as an intercessor in 1992. Nowadays, it is common to hear the word "intercessor" when I travel and visit other countries, but it was seldom heard when I first started traveling 37 years ago. Without realizing that God had called me as an intercessor, I was already teaching what intercessory prayer was, how to intercede, and its powerful effects for many years.

God's Intercessors

The following verses are just a few that show how important intercessors are to God:

> *(Isaiah 59:16)* "He saw that there was no man, and wondered that there was no intercessor; therefore, His own arm brought salvation for Him; and His own righteousness, it sustained Him."

> *(Job 9:32-33)* "For He is not a man, as I am, That I may answer Him, and that we should go to court together. Nor is there any mediator between us, who may lay his hand on us both."

(Ezekiel 22:29-31) "The people of the land have used oppressions, committed robbery, and mistreated the poor and needy; and they wrongfully oppress the stranger. So, I sought for a man among them who would make a wall and stand in the gap before Me on behalf of the land, that I should not destroy it; but I found no one. Therefore, I have poured out My indignation on them; I have consumed them with the fire of My wrath; and I have recompensed their deeds on their own heads, says the Lord GOD."

What Kind of Intercessor Is God Looking for?

1. One who can obey God's calling in their life.

Intercessors are obedient to God's call by praying according to God's purpose and plan. They will go forth with God with selflessness and sacrifice and pray for the broken families and churches. Whenever and wherever God calls them, they will stand in the gap and say, "Here I am Lord, use me as Your tool!"

2. One who can stand in the gap through intercessory prayer.

"Stand in the gap" means that we, as prayer mediators, stand in the broken places, asking God to rebuild the fallen areas of that person, church, family, or nation. Through our prayer, God relays His heart and plans to the fallen people or nation. The "broken walls" are empty places, which, in the Greek, means, "broken-down, collapsed, torn down, the crack in the wall, the gap."

The broken walls are the realm that man has given to the Devil by believing his lies and deception. In this realm, the intercessor's mission is to rebuke the enemy and fill the gap with the anointing of the Holy Spirit. This type of warfare is done in the spiritual realm, not only to renounce the Devil in Jesus' name, but also for the intercessor to firmly stand in the gap (the enemy's territory) and cast out the enemies through the power of the Holy Spirit (see 2 Corinthians 10:5). Through spiritual warfare, the intercessor can replace unforgiveness with forgiveness, hatred with love, rejection with acceptance, fear with peace, and unbelief with faith.

Standing in the gap is a term used in military warfare. It is about targeting one section of the enemy's wall to demolish and attack the city. In battle, the artillery finds the weakest section of the enemy's camp and relentlessly targets that area until it collapses. Then they invade.

Considering warfare, the soldiers who put their life on the front line are like the intercessors who are putting their life on the front line to stand in the gap. They set aside their own needs and instead pray for their broken and defeated church, family, city, or nation.

When someone is struggling to connect with God, an intercessor can help join that person with the Lord. The intercessor's prayer is like a point of connection, joining the hand of the person with the hand of God. Thus, an intercessor bridges the gap between God and the soul.

3. One who can build a spiritual wall through intercessory prayer.

The purpose of a spiritual wall is to protect the family, personal business, church, or people in need. Intercessory prayer has the power to rebuild the broken and torn-down wall. A parallel is found in the Book of Nehemiah. The city of Jerusalem was defenseless, with its walls and gates completely destroyed. In 52 days, Nehemiah rallied the people to rebuild the walls and gates, keeping their enemies at bay and keeping the people protected.

A wall collapses when the believer opens themselves up to the lies of the Devil, which allows the enemy to establish his foothold. Ephesians 4:27 tells us, *"Do not give a foothold to the devil."* The gap is a foothold, opportunity, or place where the enemy creates its territory. When we disobey or sin against God, we expose ourselves to the Devil. He can use this gap as an open door, bringing darkness and defeat to our lives. The Devil takes advantage of this foothold to attack our families, churches, cities, or nation. The enemy steals the foothold where God's people are supposed to firmly stand. Intercessors who go into spiritual warfare must pray to bring back the stolen foothold from the enemy and restore it to its original place. All of us are called to be intercessors, ones who can stand in the gap and rebuild the wall.

Today, the church has a spiritual responsibility to build a wall, a hedge of protection, around the city and local regions. If the church does not stand in the gap through intercessory prayer or repair broken walls, then sin and darkness will increase more and more, day by day. Even if churches are in every corner of a neighborhood, the results will be the same unless those churches intercede. God is looking for an intercessor, and an army of intercessors, who can rebuild the walls. All things considered, God desires to pour out healing and revival, and the work of the Holy Spirit is to restore His church and nation, and intercessors are key to making this happen.

> *(1 Timothy 2:1-4) "Therefore I exhort first of all that supplications, prayers, intercessions, and giving of thanks be made for all men, for kings and all who are in authority, that we may lead a quiet and peaceable life in all godliness and reverence. For this is good and acceptable in the sight of God our Savior, who desires all men to be saved and to come to the knowledge of the truth."*
>
> *(2 Chronicles 7:14) "If my people who are called by My name will humble themselves, and pray and seek My face, and turn from their wicked ways, then I will hear from heaven, and will forgive their sin and heal their land."*

We can build the walls through our humility and repentance. This repentance is what God requires from every intercessor.

> *(Psalm 51:9-10) "Hide Your face from my sins and blot out all my iniquities. Create in me a clean heart, O God, and renew a steadfast spirit within me."*
>
> *(Psalm 51:17) "The sacrifices of God are a broken spirit, a broken and a contrite heart—these, O God, You, will not despise."*

(James 4:6) "But He gives more grace. Therefore, He says: 'God resists the proud, but gives grace to the humble.'"

(1 Peter 5:6) "Therefore humble yourselves under the mighty hand of God, that He may exalt you in due time."

(1John 1:8-9) "If we say that we have no sin, we deceived ourselves, and the truth is not in us. If we confess our sins, He is faithful and just to forgive us our sins and to cleanse us from all unrighteousness."

When We Fill the Gap and Build the Walls

God's nature and character do not change. However, God can change His feelings and decisions toward mankind for His sovereign purpose. In the Bible, we can see how God's wrath was upon Israel, but His heart and purpose changed through one intercessor, Moses.

Throughout the Word of God, we find good reasons why God changed His heart toward a city or nation. Moses' intercessory prayer carries the assurance of God's character, purpose, and love. His intercession turned God's wrath and brought about His mercy. The favor of God was upon Moses when he prayed, even when God's people deserved to die. Through Moses' example, we can truly see the power of intercessory prayer.

(Exodus 32:11-14) "Then Moses pleaded with the Lord his God, and said: 'Lord, why does Your wrath burn hot against Your people whom You have brought out of the land of Egypt with great power and with a mighty hand? Why should the Egyptians speak, and say, 'He brought them out to harm them, to kill them in the mountains, and to consume them from the face of the earth'? Turn from Your fierce wrath and relent from this harm to Your people. Remember Abraham, Isaac, and Israel, Your servants, to whom You swore by Your own self, and said to them, 'I will multiply your descendants as the stars of heaven; and all this land that I

have spoken of I give to your descendants, and they shall inherit it forever, So the Lord relented from the harm which He said He would do to His people."

Moses reminds God that Abraham cried out to Him and desperately interceded for Sodom. God was moved by Abraham's prayer and passion. Instead of destroying the city, God revealed His mercy once again.

Genesis 18 records Abraham's prayers on behalf of Sodom. Abraham intercedes to save the wicked city and the residence of his nephew, Lot. Abraham begins asking for the corrupted city to be spared if there are but 50 righteous who are in it. He boldly prays in verse 25, *"far be it from thee to do such a thing, to slay the righteous with the wicked, so that the righteous fare as the wicked!"*

Through Abraham's interceding prayer, God was willing to change His mind. Verse 32 says, *"I will not destroy it for the sake of 10..."*

This revelation brings confident hope to intercessors.

Revival for the Last Days

The Bible foretells of a great end-times revival, where the saints are restored and renewed, preparing the way for the second coming of Jesus. God wants us to have great expectations for this revival. The purpose of revival is to bring back to life those who are spiritually dead. It is reawakening the dead in faith. It is like someone that was once blinded by fraud and deception but now able to see the truth.

God's Army Is Preparing for the Last Day Revival

On this earth, the Church is God's army. He is building His army by gathering intercessors to tear down principalities, bind forces of darkness, and foil the Devil's schemes. The people who are seeking and preparing for revival are the ones who will see it. The Lord is presently building His greatest army. This army will fight against the Devil with Him during the end times. Through these people, God will destroy and demolish the enemies' fortresses. The intercessor's calling is to bring down any stronghold that hinders God's revival.

Our enemy, the Devil, despises when intercessors pray because he knows the powerful effects of this type of prayer. The Devil also hates when God's kingdom invades the earth. For this reason, the Devil attacks and disturbs intercessors in an effort to have them cease praying. In many cases, intercessors are tormented by unknown stress and heaviness, with the goal of catching them in various calamities. The Devil likes to make God's people too busy or create difficult situations that distract intercessors from praying effectively.

As the last day revival is being prepared, the Devil's attack against the Church is intensifying. In particular, the Devil's attack against intercessors has been unmistakably fierce. Therefore, intercessors must be continually armed with spiritual discernment and be prepared to be leaders in the army for the last day's revival.

The Intercessor Who Stays Awake

(Matthew 26:41) "Watch and pray, that ye enter not into temptation!"

This verse does not mean that you must close your eyes and kneel to pray. "Watch and pray" means to be careful. When we are awake—physically and spiritually—when troubles arise, we will have the discernment to resist temptation. Being awake allows us to also hear God's voice and understand His will. This awareness allows us to be more vigilant, and sensitive to our surroundings.

If we are not fully awake, it's like a person getting up in the morning before having their first cup of coffee. They are still drowsy, half asleep, and unable to hear God's voice. If we do not hear God's voice clearly, we can be confused, even after praying.

Oftentimes, we hear an inner voice or Satan's accusations, mistaking it for God's voice. Some people insist that they pray a lot, but don't have spiritual discernment, and many times are speaking out of their "flesh." For example, one person says, "God told me that you are supposed to be a missionary." The problem is that God never told the other person! Normally, the prophetic voice is a witness and confirmation to the person's heart regarding what God already has shown or is dealing with. So, the first person speaking on behalf of God doesn't know what they are talking about. They may also easily fall into temptation over very small matters. Only when we are awake—physically and spiritually—can we have a clear mind, able to carefully discern between the voice of our flesh and the voice of the Devil.

The Lord sees and hears what we cannot see or hear. The gift and blessing of an intercessor is the ability to hear God's voice and discern between spirit and natural. As intercessors, we cannot allow ourselves to fall into Satan's temptations. This will hinder the effectiveness of our prayers. Furthermore, as mediators who glorify God, we must be willing to joyfully intercede and fill in the gap.

Those Who Distract the Revival

The Devil is not the only one who distracts intercessors from preparing for God's revival. It can also be religious people at church. A religious person is one who honors God with their lips, but does not seek Him deeply within their heart. Religious people know how to act, talk, or seem "spiritual" but have no real relationship with the Lord. Additionally, these people claim they are experiencing the "anointing of God," yet their words lack any true evidence or power to support their experience. Even the unsaved are often aware of these religious people, and because of them they want no part of Jesus.

(Isaiah 29:13) "Therefore the Lord said: "In as much as these people draw near with their mouths and honor Me with their lips,

but have removed their hearts far from Me, and their fear toward Me is taught by the commandment of men."

(Ezekiel 33:30-32) "As for you, son of man, the children of your people are talking about you beside the walls and in the doors of the houses; and they speak to one another, everyone saying to his brother, 'Please come and hear what the word is that comes from the Lord.' So, they come to you as people do, they sit before you as My people, and they hear your words, but they do not do them; for with their mouth, they show much love, but their hearts pursue their own gain. Indeed, you are to them as a very lovely song of one who has a pleasant voice and can play well on an instrument; for they hear your words, but they do not do them."

A Religious Person Is Someone:

- who thinks of themselves as "spiritual"
- who thinks, "I am praying more than others"
- who wants to gain attention from others
- who is prideful and conceited
- who is boastful and filled with self-righteousness
- who fears man more than God
- who carries fear and insecurity

These people care more about how they are perceived by others, rather than what God thinks about them. In contrast, a truly sincere and faithful person is not hindered by what people think of them. They only think about how to glorify God through their life and service.

(Matthew 6:5-8) "And when you pray, you shall not be like the hypocrites. For they love to pray to stand in the synagogues and on the corners of the streets, that they may be seen by men. Assuredly, I say to you, they have their reward. But you, when you pray, go into your room, and when you have shut your door, pray to your Father

who is in the secret place; and your Father who sees in secret will reward you openly. And when you pray, do not use vain repetitions as the heathen do. For they think that they will be heard for their many words. "Therefore. do not be like them. For your Father knows the things you need of before you ask Him."

The Spotless and Whole Church

God is preparing for the second coming of Jesus Christ and the final outpouring of the Holy Spirit upon His church. To pour out the Holy Spirit, He is searching those who are willing to completely surrender to Him, to follow His will, and say, "Yes Lord; whatever you desire." God desires His Church—His Body and the Bride of Christ—to be whole and untainted, so He deals with our inner man first. He wants to remove our unrighteousness and wash away our impurity and iniquities. This transformation process is not going to be easy.

As we are freed and healed from the wounds and yokes that bind us, we become more like Christ. The Lord's glory appears through us, and demons tremble. The power of darkness will flee when the Church shines with God's glory. When we receive the revelation of Who lives within us, the darkness fades away.

> *(1 John 4:4) "You are of God, little children, and have overcome them, because He who is in you is greater than he who is in the world."*

> *(1 Thessalonians 5:23) "Now may the God of peace Himself sanctify you completely; and may your whole spirit, soul, and body be preserved blameless at the coming of our Lord Jesus Christ."*

> *(1 Peter 3:12) "For the eyes of the Lord are on the righteous, and His ears are open to their prayers, but the face of the Lord is against those who do evil."*

> *(2 Corinthians 3:18) "But we all, with unveiled face, beholding as in a mirror the glory of the Lord, are being transformed into the same image from glory to glory, just as by the Spirit of the Lord."*

CHAPTER 2

A TESTIMONY TO
THE POWER OF INTERCESSORY PRAYER

The following is a true testimony to the power of intercessory prayer. For 15 years our church has had a special couple named John and Linda. John was an intercessor and Linda was a worship leader. When John was led by the Holy Spirit, his prayers touched and encouraged many. Unfortunately, he had a serious problem. He served in the Vietnam War and killed many people. Because of that, he had deep wounds within his soul.

Every now and then, he would blow up and change into a completely different person. He would burst out and say that he would kill everyone. Although, we continued to pray for his wounded heart for over 15 years, my late husband, Pastor Larry, and I were drained by the burden of John's condition.

They had seven children including twins, so Linda did not work outside their home. John received monthly benefits from the government because he had picked up a rare skin disease during his tour in the Vietnam War. Although, he received government help, they always faced financial hardship. John had difficulty keeping any job for more than six months. As a result, they repeatedly asked for financial help from our church for their rent and electricity bills. Whether it is true or not, we felt that they began to believe that the church was responsible for their needs. At that time, the church was not financially stable, but we helped, even if it meant sacrificing our salary.

Lay down your heavy burdens

One day, my late husband, Pastor Larry, and I were praying for this family, and we received the same confirmation from God. He said, "You have worked hard, now release them to Me and give Me your heavy burdens. And do not feel responsible for their financial needs anymore."

We both heard such a clear voice from God that we could not ignore it. Finally, we told John and Linda that we could not support them anymore. As soon as we told them, John stood up and exploded with anger. He yelled at the top of his lungs and out of his lips gushed unimaginable words against the church and us.

For more than 15 years, I had prayed for John with many tears, but as I witnessed this rage my heart began to harden toward him. From that moment on, I prayed more formally but could not intercede with a sincere heart.

I could not easily let go of the pain that I received from John that day, and it turned to bitterness within me. This opened the door for the Devil to accuse and ridicule me. It became a constant distraction, and I was no longer able to pray or intercede for John. The disappointment and discouragement that I accumulated for the last 15 years now filled my heart with hatred and anger. Gradually, I distanced myself, knowing we could no longer help John as his pastors. I thought, *"How dare you treat us this way after all that we've done for you and your family?"* No matter how much I tried to let go of the pain in my heart, it remained unresolved.

Exhausted

A couple of weeks after that incident, I received a phone call from Linda and her voice was full of desperation. She said, "Pastor Sun, John blew up last night! He was walking around the house with a knife, cutting the curtains and sofa, saying that he would kill all of us! I had no choice but to call the police to remove him from the house. He was violent at times in the past, but this time it was way too much and was extremely dangerous."

Linda was crying so hard that she could hardly breathe. She continued, "Yesterday, the police put John in the veteran's hospital. But today, I received a call from him saying that whenever he returns home, he will kill everyone in the house. What should we do?! Pastor Sun, I'm so scared, please help us!"

Hearing Linda's cry for help, I told her to meet me at church. As soon as she saw me, she ran to me and hugged me, putting her head on my shoulder, and sobbing. Strangely, I did not have any emotion or tears; instead, I started praying in tongues only through my lips and patted Linda's back. Usually, I am a person who easily cries, because I have a compassionate heart for people in need. But this time, my heart was shut down. My mind was telling me to cry with Linda, to comfort her, but there were no feelings of empathy in my heart for her. There were similar situations in the last 15 years when John would blow up, but this time, it was the most serious. However, I was already exhausted emotionally, in addition to the bitterness I had towards John. I was only able to pray for poor Linda, giving her a few words of comfort and encouragement before returning home.

Date Night or Intercession Night?

That night, my late husband and I had planned to go on a date. It had been a while since we spent some quality time together, due to our busy schedules. We had already set the date and time for a special evening a couple of months prior.

When we were ready to leave, I received a phone call from Linda: "Pastor Sun, John called me again! He said that he will be discharged tomorrow and when he comes home, he will kill all of us. The kids and I are very scared right now! I am sorry but could you please come by my house to pray for us? Will you please?"

I did not want to hear her voice. I murmured to myself, "What more do you want from us? Isn't it enough that we have already sacrificed 15 years for your family?"

At this point, I couldn't find even the smallest amount of sympathy for John. In my heart, I reasoned making any kind of excuse to avoid going to her house.

Right then, my husband. Pastor Larry asked, "Who called?" I already told him about Linda and John's story earlier in the day.

I said, "Linda called me again." Then, I started complaining to him. "Linda and John's problems and situations are never ending, and it makes me very tired. John and Linda are asking for the same prayer requests all the time; let's not worry about her right now. Let us just go out as we had planned to do." My heart was cold and extremely hard at this point.

My husband responded, "Sun, do you think we can have a good time on our date, if we go out like this? Let's postpone our date and go to Linda's house to pray for her family."

Before he even said this, my heart was already uneasy and uncomfortable about going out. I nodded my head, and said, "Okay. We can briefly drop by her house and pray, but when I give you a sign, promise me that you will allow us to leave. If it's not too late after praying for Linda, let's go on our date."

The Clear Voice of God

When we arrived at Linda's house, it looked like a battlefield. Linda was so depressed, she still had not cleaned the chaos that John had made the night before. As I walked around the house, it looked like it had been hit by a tornado. As a woman, I genuinely felt sorry for Linda and her children because of what they were going through. I grabbed Linda's hand, squeezing it tightly, praying for God to show His mercy upon her and the children, who were suffering so much. I was praying but still had no emotions, tears, or compassion.

After we had finished praying, I gave a sign to my husband for us to leave. Surprisingly, he instead gave me a sign to stay put. When I looked at Pastor Larry, he was listening intensely to Linda's melancholy story. I thought, *I guess this evening's date is over.* I barely managed to hide my disappointed heart, and stared at Linda while she cried and complained about her marriage. After what seemed like forever, we prayed for her one last time, and stood up to leave. I glanced at the clock and it seemed that we still had time for our date, so I rushed to say goodbye.

As I walked towards the front door to leave, suddenly I heard a voice saying, "Don't go." I looked back at my husband, thinking that it was him. I asked, "What did you say?"

My husband said, "I didn't say anything."

I stepped forward towards the front door, and again, I heard the same voice: "Don't go!" This time it was much louder. Instinctively, I knew this was God's voice.

Suddenly, I felt my whole body become frozen, and I stood there like someone who had completely lost their mind. God kept speaking to my heart: "If you leave now, you will be defeated and regret it later! If you intercede for this family with a sincere heart before you leave, then you will be victorious!"

I had to make a quick decision on whether to go out on our date or sacrifice this time to pray. Even though I knew what God wanted me to do, I still asked, "God, what do you want from me?"

"Stay and pray for this family."

"How should I pray for this family?"

"Ask for oil from Linda and pray for this house."

I looked at Linda and asked her to give me some olive oil, if she had any in the house. When Linda brought the oil in a small bowl, I said God wants us to apply this oil to every corner of the house before we leave. I asked her to guide us through the entire house. We anointed the house while we prayed in tongues, casting out all evil spirits.

The Moment the Holy Spirit Holds On

As we were guided by Linda, we applied the oil throughout the house and prayed in tongues. Linda's house was two stories; we finished praying and applying the oil on the first floor, then we moved on to the second floor.

When we went up to the second floor, Linda explained that the first room was her thirteen-year-old daughter's room. Suddenly, my heart was stirred up and I felt the Holy Spirit upon me. At that moment, their daughter's image appeared in front of me, and I felt a strong impression that she was contemplating suicide, because of the hurts and wounds she received from her dad. I felt so bad for John's daughter, and I felt the grief and mourning of God's heart.

All of a sudden, I couldn't bear it, because my heart was in much sorrow and anguish. I walked into the middle of the room and sat on the floor and began to wail out of control with tears. I was travailing and praying with the same pain as if I were delivering a baby. Throughout the years of my ministry, I had experienced travailing prayers often, so I knew at that moment what was going on. All I could do let myself go and let Holy Spirit have His way.

Although it is painful when giving birth to a baby, we find great joy after the delivery and so is travailing prayer. Just as we forget all the painful moments, immediately after embracing our newborn baby, the outcome of a travailing prayer with sacrifice and devotion will give great joy and peace to us.

The Vision God Showed

I was in a spiritual battle, travailing with prayer diligently for about thirty minutes. During the prayer, I saw a vision of myself standing in the middle of a battlefield. There were countless enemies walking back and forth, lingering in front of me, persistently accusing me and mocking me. I was agitated and extremely disturbed by them. Then, I swung the sword that I was holding in my hand at the enemy, and I killed them all.

The Price of Obedience

As the travailing prayer gradually ended, my heart, that was once closed, finally opened. I felt peace and the joy of the Lord was restored upon me.

The feeling of the absolute peace of God was like a strong current of a waterfall being poured upon my head and it gave me such refreshment and excitement. This gave me an unspeakable joy, like nothing else in the world matters. My heart was thrilled with the thought of executing all the enemies that accused and mocked me; I knew I had a total victory on that battlefield.

Since I had an awesome spiritual breakthrough in their daughter's room, my steps were lighter and I could not stop saying, "Praise God! I love you, Lord! Thank You, Jesus!" I repeated these words over and over, then finished praying through the entire house. However, a strange and surprising thing happened to me, as we were walking around the second floor and heading down the stairs. All the hatred and bitterness I had towards John instantly disappeared. Instead, tears were shed endlessly, because of the compassion I felt towards him. I was barely able to control my emotions.

I was about to leave the house after the last prayer, when the Holy Spirit amazed me once again. I thought my duty was over, but the Holy Spirit was not done yet. The unexpected repentance that came without notice startled me. I surrendered completely to His amazing and relentless love immediately, as I realized God's absolute patience and faithfulness toward John and me. I was deeply sorry and embarrassed before the Lord for being stubborn, and not forgiving John sooner. "God, I'm sorry. I was wrong. Please forgive me," I prayed in my heart as I covered my face with my two hands and cried.

Since I kept sobbing without saying anything, my confused husband said, "Honey, if you are done with prayers then let's go."

Then I was able to control my emotions, and said to Linda, "When I was praying for your family, God gave me a great spiritual breakthrough.

So do not worry about anything, just trust in God. His miracle will be upon your house."

Finally, after giving thanks to God, we left Linda's house.

My Unforgettable Testimony

When I got into the car and checked the time, it was 7 o'clock. We arrived at Linda's house at 5 o'clock, but thankfully it was not too late to enjoy the date with my husband.

That evening was incredibly special, fresher, and more exciting than the other dates we have been on. I was unable to fully express the overwhelming joy that came through intercession, which demolished the strongholds, principalities, and the power of darkness that oppressed that family.

The Devil took advantage of me because of the bitterness, hatred, and anger that I had towards John, and that had opened the door for the Devil to relentlessly accuse and mock me. It hindered me from interceding for John and his family, and inhibited me from bearing God's beautiful calling and intercession. However, when urgent circumstances arose, the price of obedience exceeded my imagination, and it became an unforgettable testimony for the rest of my life (see Isaiah 1:19). Through that time of intercessory prayer, the Holy Spirit caused me to acknowledge my injustice and sin, which convicted me to repent, restoring within me the childlike faith and fresh love of God, which had been stolen by the Devil. Once again, I give my everlasting gratitude and glory to God, who moved my heart to intercede for John and Linda's family in their time of desperate need.

Flipping the Devil's Scheme

I came to know the price of my obedience and sacrifice the following day.

John called Linda early in the morning. "Linda, something strange happened to me last night. All-day long in the hospital room, I was scared and shook in fear. But around seven o'clock last night, God visited me, and the Holy Spirit brought a strong conviction over me to repent of my sin. Linda, I know how terrible of a husband and father I have been. I have done so many horrible things to you; please forgive me. I do not deserve to be your husband, and if you do not want me, I will not hate you. I have done terrible things to you and I know now it is all my fault. I only want your forgiveness."

"I do not even deserve to be loved by you, and it is only because of God's grace that I am breathing right now. What have I done to God, to you, and our children? How did I do such evil things to my own family? I have committed great sins before God; I want God to forgive me. And if you forgive and accept me again, then I will be good to you and the children, for the rest of my life."

According to Linda, he had never cried so hard in his life, nor did he ever apologize for his mistakes before. Since returning home, he never said anything again about killing his family. Later, he met with my husband and me and apologized for all his wrongdoings in the past, wanting to be forgiven, and sincerely asked for reconciliation.

The result of intercession by listening to God's voice and obeying Him had reversed the Devil's plan to steal the happiness of John's family, and to destroy and kill them (see John 10:10). Instead, through the sincere prayer of intercession, the Devil was defeated. God showed us the beautiful miracle of restoring a broken family and building them up. Amazingly, at 7 o'clock, the same time we finished the prayer and left the house, God visited John and transformed his heart 180 degrees.

To My Readers

You may be thinking, *Do I experience spiritual breakthrough only when I cry out like Pastor Sun and offer a travailing prayer?*

I want to reassure you that is not the case, and I would like to say a few things that will help you.

When we are praying for ourselves or interceding for others, it is most important for us to be sensitive to the Holy Spirit's voice and obey it. So many intercessors have asked me the same questions, but my answer is the same, every time. We all have different characters and styles. Since we have different personalities, the way that the Holy Spirit deals with each of us will vary. Some women give birth with tears, sweat, and screams, while other women with their lips tightly closed, swallowing their tears, and quietly moaning. Intercessors who are travailing are the same way. Also, what we must understand is that our reactions are different, depending on the case and situation. As long as we have a heart of obedience towards our Lord's will, the Holy Spirit will guide us to the path He desires, whenever, wherever, and in whatever method. We never know how God is going to respond to our prayer, or how He is going to deal with us. This is because our situation will not be the same every time.

Prayer of Faith More Than Emotional Prayer

It is a misconception to believe that we have prayed well if we cry, and it is less powerful if there were no tears. This was a truth in my life until God trained me.

Before I believed in Jesus, I was the type of person who cried a lot. However, after I met Jesus, I cried even more than before. I cried while reading the Bible, praying, worshipping, and even when I saw homeless people. I cried especially when I prayed for someone, because I could feel their hurts and pain. It was to the extent that I could not pray without tears. Because I cried so much and so often, it embarrassed me at times.

When I asked my spiritual leaders, they said this was because of my emotional sensitivity and that there was nothing to worry about. However, there was a period of time when the tears did not come as frequently as before, and I became very worried.

For a while, I lost confidence in my prayer. Then one day, I cried out and asked Jesus, "Lord, examine me. What is wrong with me? Do I have an unknown sin in my life? Any root of bitterness blocking my prayer? Lord, you know the great and mighty secrets which I do not know, so please show me."

Finally, the Holy Spirit spoke to me: "When you pray, do not judge your prayers as good or bad based on whether you cried or did not cry. And do not be assured that every time I see your tears then I will answer your prayers every time. Rather than depending on your prayer that is mixed with tears and emotions, I want you to pray that you can always come to me with wholehearted faith and meet Me with humility and an open heart."

Surely, God was teaching. Sometimes we pray with tears, but it is wrong to think that prayer is only good when there are always tears. I needed to have complete faith in God, rather than trust my emotions. Without me knowing, I was making a religious law called "only tearful prayers are good and powerful." Misconceptions, wrong beliefs, and ideas can open the door for us to easily be deceived and fall into a religious mindset.

It has been 46 years since I met Jesus, and I have served Him as my Lord and Savior to the best of my ability. He knew I was a person who was easily swayed by my emotions. Therefore, He taught me early on about fasting and trained me to deny and die to myself, as He showed me His power and endless love. Even to this day, God wants to show and teach me truths that I have not yet realized, because of my own ignorance. Although I do not know when I'm going to see Jesus face to face, I hope to continue having an open heart to receive His teachings, so that I can become a balanced intercessor who isn't moved solely by emotions.

CHAPTER 3

WHAT IS INTERCESSORY PRAYER?

The Prayer that Pleases God

There are many types of prayers, such as the prayer of intercession, prayer of fasting, meditation prayer, warfare prayer, audible
prayer, praying in tongues, the prayer of faith, word of prayer, declaration
prayer, congregational prayer, agreement of prayer, travailing prayer, seasonal prayer, devotional prayer, early morning prayer, all-night prayer, and
others. Of course, there is no doubt in my mind that God delights and is
pleased to receive *all* our prayers. However, what I am about to tell you,
you may not agree with, but I can only speak of my conviction from the
Holy Spirit. I believe that the Lord delights in the prayer of intercession
more than any other prayers.

In the past, I strongly believed that fasting and prayer was the
prayer that God was pleased with the most, because it takes denying and
crucifying the flesh. I experienced many of its great effects. From 1986 to
1996, God led me countless times and has trained me intensely through
fasting.

Once I finished one fast, I felt to go on another to continually crucify my flesh and be healed of deep wounds that were in my soul. I
needed lots of inner healing, and I also needed to discipline my flesh
under the authority of God through fasting. Through fasting, the Lord

continuously led me to surrender myself to His rule and control over my thoughts, greed, lust, and desires for worldly things.

In 1992, I published a book on prayer and fasting. God led me to write a teaching book with my testimony on various lessons learned from fasting, and how I came to know Jesus more personally. For a long time, I insisted and taught that God is pleased with prayer and fasting more than any other type of prayer. But as the years passed and I received more revelations from the Holy Spirit, and learned much more about intercessory prayer and its powers, I can now say with full confidence and boldness that the prayer God is most pleased with is the intercessory prayer. (Again, I can only speak out of my own experience, not "thus saith the Lord.")

Why Is God so Pleased with Intercessory Prayer?

The reason why I say God is pleased with intercessory prayer is that, when I look back on all the years of my personal prayer life, there were many times that I fasted and prayed only to find a solution for *my* problems and to deny *myself* for the purpose *personal* transformation. Of course, at times I prayed and fasted for others, the church, and the nation. But to be honest, I prayed and fasted much more for my own needs.

In contrast, intercessors pray to God with 100 percent dedication, sacrificing their time to pray for other people, their church, and their nation. God's Kingdom principle is *giving*. God *gave* His only son Jesus to save mankind (John 3:16-17). Jesus *gave* His life for our salvation. The Holy Spirit *testifies* of the glory of Jesus (John 15:26). When our loved ones are sick or faced with financial hardship, surrounded by a difficult situation, or the church is being oppressed by the forces of darkness and the nation is in chaos, intercessors want to do something. But when we cannot heal the one who is dying, and we feel frustrated not being able to personally help those in need, this is when the intercessor stands in the gap and trusts God to take care of their loved one's needs.

A Prayer that Cannot be Done without Self-Sacrifice

Intercessors must put other people's needs above their own. We cannot intercede for others, unless we give our full dedication and sacrifice.

Intercessors can pray in front of people, but normally they pray in a secret place that nobody knows of to spend more time with the Lord. Therefore, the Lord is pleased with this mediator who prays for their neighbors, church, and nation with a sincere and earnest heart, and is unshaken even if they are not praised or acknowledged by others. As a result, God pours out special favor and blessing upon them.

> *(Matthew 6:6) "But you, when you pray, go into your room, and when you have shut your door, pray to your Father who is in the secret place; and your Father who sees in secret will reward you openly."*

Mediator's Role: Intercessory Prayer

Intercessory prayer is the work of a mediator. The Bible is very clear that Jesus *"ever lives to make intercession for us"* (Hebrews 7:25). We cannot find God ourselves, and without the help of Jesus, we cannot receive salvation on our own (John 14:6). Here on earth, intercessors play a key role God's sovereign work in the lives of those who are not believers and Christians alike.

> *(1 Timothy 2:5) "For there is one God and one mediator between God and mankind, the man Christ Jesus."*

This verse tells us the role of a mediator. As intercessors, we partner with God to intercede on behalf of others as He leads. While God sovereignly reveals Himself as times to individuals, most often He looks for someone to intercede in order for Him to do the work of salvation He desires to do.

An Intercessor Is a Watchman

> *(Nehemiah 4:7-9) "Now it happened, when Sanballat, Tobiah, the Arabs, the Ammonites, and the Ashdodites heard that the walls of Jerusalem were being restored and the gaps were beginning to be closed, that they became very angry, and all of them conspired together to come and attack Jerusalem and create confusion. Nevertheless, we made our prayer to our God, and because of them we set a watch against them day and night."*

Reconstructing the wall means to protect from outside attacks. Sanballat and Tobias knew that the Israelites were reconstructing the wall and they wanted to stop them from rebuilding it, and they planned to attack Jerusalem. This demonstrates that our common enemy, demonic spirits, can attack broken homes, churches, cities, and nations because they know our weaknesses and the open gaps. To prevent the enemy from entering the city, Nehemiah set a watchman on the wall while it was still being built, day and night.

Today's intercessor must be the "watchman" over families, church, city, and nation to prevent the Devil's cohorts from taking advantage of the open gaps. The "broken walls" in our lives bring spiritual defeat. In the book of Nehemiah, the broken wall around the city allowed their enemies to trample freely on God's people. In the same way, spiritually broken walls allow for the enemy to trample on God's people, His church, and society at large.

> *(Ephesians 4:27) "nor give place to the devil."*
>
> *(Ecclesiastes 10:8) "He who digs a pit will fall into it, and whoever breaks through a wall will be bitten by a serpent."*
>
> *(Isaiah 5:5) "And now, please let Me tell you what I will do to My vineyard: I will take away its hedge, and it shall be burned; and break down its wall, and it shall be trampled down."*

(Psalm 80:12) "Why have You broken down her hedges, so that all who pass by the way pluck her fruit?

Having the Heart of God

Intercessory prayer is a watchman's prayer. With the heart of God, it is a prayer that penetrates the Devil's attack and resists it.

How can we have the heart of God when offering intercessory prayer?

First, we must empty of ourselves. Our hearts must be emptied to be filled with the Spirit of God. Then, through the heart of God, who is all-knowing, we can know our neighbor's pain, and we can more effectively intercede for them. Next, we must learn when the enemy is attacking us, to quickly discern his tactics, and submit every negative thought that is against the word of God. Then we can pull down the strongholds of the enemy (2 Corinthians 10:3-5). Finally, we must be sensitive to the leading of the Holy Spirit, and resist bringing in worldly things into our hearts and minds. The worldly things diminish our discernment. If we are double-minded, we cannot hear the Holy Spirit's voice (James 1:7-8).

CHAPTER 4

JESUS IS OUR MEDIATOR

Jesus, Our Mediator

God's intercessors must follow the example of Jesus Christ, the ultimate mediator, who demonstrated intercession. One of Jesus' ministries is intercessory prayer. Even after Jesus resurrected and ascended, to this day, he continues to intercede for the church at the seat on the right hand of God.

> *(1 Timothy 2:5) "For there is one God and one Mediator between God and men, the Man Christ Jesus."*
>
> *(Romans 8:34) "Who is he who condemns? It is Christ who died, and furthermore is also risen, who is even at the right hand of God, who also makes intercession for us."*
>
> *(1 John 2:1) "My little children, these things I write to you, so that you may not sin. And if anyone sins, we have an Advocate with the Father, Jesus Christ the righteous."*

Jesus, Our Advocate

The mediator is expressed as an advocate, and an advocate is a lawyer. If I commit a crime and stand in court, a lawyer defends me so that I receive fair justice and, hopefully, the least amount of punishment. Taking that into consideration, Jesus knows how to intercede for us according to God's will.

It is extremely important, what kind of lawyer we choose. Unless I am foolish, I would not ask for help from a person who is an alcoholic, drug addict, lacking in character, or unfaithful in their marriage. Can I have confidence in their ability? Will they truly help me? Will there be power in the words of my lawyer?

The lawyer who stands on behalf of us must know the law and be able to defend us, while standing boldly before a judge. We would not hire an attorney who does not know the law, is not confident in winning, and has a bad reputation on our side.

Jesus is the perfect attorney, who knows every jot and tittle of the law. He knows all about our circumstances and situation in every detail and knows every detail of God's will.

Jesus, the Perfect Attorney

Nothing is more perfect than having Jesus as our attorney to defend us before God. No one can defend us better than Jesus. Although people can fail, Jesus will never fail; He will never leave us or forsake us (Hebrews 13:5). We are hidden in Christ; therefore, God sees us through Christ (Colossians 3:3). When we are heading towards the wrong path, Jesus defends us before God and gives us the opportunity to restore our relationship with God. It is because of Jesus' blood and His atoning sacrificial life that we can stand before God the Father. Furthermore, we can come before God boldly and confidently saying, "God, here I am."

As the Word says, *"If we acknowledge and confess our sins, He is faithful to forgive and cleanse us from all unrighteousness"* (1 John 1:9). We are bestowed with a special favor, because Jesus offered Himself as a propitiation for us (Hebrews 10:1-22).

> *(Hebrews 10:10) "By that will we have been sanctified through the offering of the body of Jesus Christ once for all."*

(Hebrews 10:17) "Their sins and their lawless deeds I will remember no more."

(Hebrews 9:22) "...without shedding of blood there is no remission."

(Hebrews 10:19) "Therefore, brethren, having boldness to enter the Holiest by the blood of Jesus."

It is the greatest blessing that all our injustices and sins can be washed away by Jesus' blood, and we can find favor to stand boldly before God's throne.

(Hebrews 4:15-16) "For we do not have a High Priest who cannot sympathize with our weaknesses, but was in all points tempted as we are, yet without sin. Let us, therefore, come boldly to the throne of grace, that we may obtain mercy and find grace to help in time of need."

Jesus came as a man from heaven to show us His Father God and make known to us His revelation. Through His death and resurrection, He made a way for us to encounter God.

(John 14:6) "Jesus said to him, 'I am the way, the truth, and the life. No one comes to the Father except through Me.'"

Jesus' Intercession for Us

Many people say, "One day, I just decided to believe in God." Although we may feel like we just decided to believe in Jesus by ourselves, in truth, someone was in the middle. We were able to come to God because of someone who prayed for or evangelized us. We cannot come to God in our strength. Jesus filled in the gap between God and us. He became the Way, the Truth, and the Life for us; through Him, we have an open relationship with Father God.

Jesus Christ is the mediator who unconditionally loves us and is constantly interceding for us. If Jesus does not intercede for us, we will never receive salvation. Because we are inadequate and vulnerable, Jesus knows how much we need God in every moment. Because Jesus intercedes for us without ceasing, we have everlasting life, we come to the throne of God to receive grace and find mercy, and we have the conviction of the Holy Spirit to keep us on the straight and narrow.

If Jesus only prayed for us to obtain our salvation and ended it there, how could we overcome our daily sufferings, pains, trials, and tests? Because Jesus wants us to draw closer to God and daily grow our maturity in Him, He continues to intercede for us even today. Just because we received salvation does not mean that all our problems are gone, and we become whole and perfect on the spot. How wonderful would it be if we could declare daily that we are perfect and have no problems whatsoever? Because of the sin in our lives every day, we need someone's intercession. For this reason, we are transformed through Jesus' intercession, and we can have the inspiration and counsel of the Holy Spirit.

Resembling the Character and Image of Jesus

We do not live in a clean and perfect state, even after we get saved. Whether we know it or not, we tend to sin again and again. Many times, we express anger that is displeasing to God. Wouldn't it be nice to think that we could stand before God as a whole and perfect person every day of our lives, just because we received Jesus Christ as our Savior? When we receive salvation by faith through grace (Ephesians 2:8-9), we must continue to spiritually transform daily, consistently denying ourselves, and practice self-control. Through the power of the Holy Spirit, we put off our bad habits, injustices, and negative attitudes one by one. The Holy Spirit also empowers us to resemble the character and image of Jesus Christ.

(Ephesians 4:17-24) "This I say, therefore, and testify in the Lord, that you should no longer walk as the rest of the Gentiles walk, in

the futility of their mind, having their understanding darkened, being alienated from the life of God, because of the ignorance that is in them, because of the blindness of their heart; who, being past feeling, have given themselves over to lewdness, to work all uncleanness with greediness. But you have not so learned Christ, if indeed you have heard Him and have been taught by Him, as the truth is in Jesus: that you put off, concerning your former conduct, the old man which grows corrupt according to the deceitful lusts, and be renewed in the spirit of your mind, and that you put on the new man which was created according to God, in true righteousness and holiness."

(Philippians 2:12) "Therefore, my beloved, as you have always obeyed, not as in my presence only, but now much more in my absence, work out your own salvation with fear and trembling."

(Romans 8:33) "Who shall bring a charge against God's elect? It is God who justifies."

CHAPTER 5

THE POWER OF INTERCESSORY PRAYER TESTIMONY: MY BEAUTIFUL GRANDCHILDREN

Apples of My Eye

My oldest son, Jody, lived with his ex-wife, Heather, for ten years and divorced. The testimony I am going to tell you happened a a few years before their divorce. They have three beautiful children and I love them so much; I've always said I was the happiest grandma in the whole world. I always boast about them everywhere I go. However, the saddest thing for our family was, unfortunately, Jody's ex-wife was a drug addict.

Before marriage, Heather had a drug problem, but my son did not know it at the time and this truth was later found out. When Heather gave birth to her third child and developed a female organ problem, she was admitted to the hospital for a big operation. Even after the operation, she frequently visited the hospital for many more procedures before finally coming to a place where she could not take care of her children anymore. Due to her illness, the children were left at my house almost all the time. That had concerned me a lot, not because the children were living with me, but their family situation had concerned me more. One day, to my surprise, I heard the news that Heather asked her mother to take care of my precious grandbabies. Later I found out that since Heather felt bad asking me to take care of her children so frequently, she asked her mother for help without discussing this with me. Heather's mother lived in another state about three hours away from us.

An Innocent Mistake Became a Disaster

Sadly, Jody and Heather accidentally made a huge mistake in signing documents that they thought were giving temporary guardianship of their children to Heather's mother. They were told the guardianship was needed to care for the kids while they were living in another state. The content of the document gave full legal right of guardianship, which caused a serious legal problem later. Jody and Heather were young, and they trusted Heather's mother without any question. But surprisingly she had another plan. I was shocked and greatly disappointed when I heard this news. Soon after, Heather's mother called me and wanted to come to my house to take away my beautiful grandbabies.

The Decision of Heather's Mother

Despite Heather's mother objecting to Jody and Heather's marriage, they both insisted on getting married. Therefore, their marriage started without the acceptance and blessing of Heather's mother. From the very beginning, they received no support from Heather's mother. Even after several years of marriage, she never acknowledged my son as her son-in-law.

Thankfully, despite Heather's drug problem, she gave birth to two beautiful daughters and the cutest son, ages five, three, and one.

Occasionally, Heather's mother heard of her daughter's struggles, and she worried about the kids; she was afraid the children weren't receiving proper care. When Heather reached out for help, her mother thought this was the best opportunity and her only chance to get the kids. So, she tricked Jody and Heather into signing a document that legally forfeited their guardianship of the children.

Heather's Mother Calls

One day, Heather's mother called me to say she was coming to take the kids. In truth, I was a busy person and had a pile of work to do, but I was in a situation where I had to take care of my grandchildren and was thankful it was only temporary. My son's house was not too far away, so whenever the children's mother fainted from drug usage, or whenever they had a family problem, the children were used to coming over to my house. However, after hearing the details from Heather's mother of what was going to happen, I was so shocked that I felt like I got hit with a hammer on the head. I was shaking uncontrollably, then I asked my son, who was standing by me, "What is going on?"

Jody explained that he and Heather's mistake was not understanding the documents thoroughly, and trusting Heather's mother. No matter how he explained it to me, it was extremely hard to understand why this was happening. The thought of the senseless and foolish actions of my son and daughter-in-law made me incredibly angry. But there was no time to even think about my feelings.

In a state of much confusion and frustration, I barely calmed down after the terrible news. I called Heather's mother and I pleaded with tears; this was not a good idea, and I could take good care of them. "Please don't take away the children who are living comfortably in our home right now," I pleaded.

But she said, "I am on my way to pick up my grandchildren and will be there in the next three hours. Please get my grandchildren ready for me."

No matter how much I told her about how the kids were extremely anxious, since they are frequently separated from their parents, she didn't want to listen. She stubbornly insisted that she would even come with the police, if necessary.

Bewildered Grandchildren

Due to the long distance to Heather's mother's house, the children did not visit her often, and did not have a close relationship with her. My heart was constantly beating with anxiety. I barely restrained my trembling heart when I told the children they will be visiting their other Grandma's house for a while, and that they would shortly return. But no matter how much I tried to calm and persuade them, they were afraid of leaving me. It was not because it was her house, but anywhere they went they felt anxious. My grandchildren would often say that my house was the best and they wanted to live forever with us. Though they did not know anything about the situation, the children somehow sensed that something was not right.

Suddenly, my oldest, five-year-old granddaughter began to cry, saying, "I won't go to my other grandmother's house." Then my three-year-old granddaughter started to cry, saying that she would not go either. My youngest, one-year-old grandson joined them, crying uncontrollably and all three kids were hanging on to me. I felt like my heart was collapsing as I watched my grandchildren wailing and sobbing. Then Heather's mother called, saying she was close to my house. My heart was racing. No matter how much I tried to explain to my babies, they were too young to understand. They hid in the closet, then under their beds, then made the wildest commotion because they did not want to go.

Anxiety and Fear Tightens My Heart

I felt like a person without a soul, watching the bewildered children, when suddenly it felt like anxiety and fear were strangling my lungs. I felt I could not even breathe. I walked into the downstairs room, then over to the corner, and sat down. I curled up and prayed to God. I was zoned out and so weak that no matter how much I called on God, no sound came out of my mouth. Even though I called and searched for my God with all my strength, I could not sense Him. I was searching for an answer but only my grandbabies lingered in front of my eyes. I was so afraid and anxious that I could only repeat the same words, "Oh Lord … What should I do?" and I felt like my body kept shrinking.

A Sudden Reminder of Intercessory Prayer

Suddenly, a thought quickened in my mind: *Aren't you supposed to be praying for your Bishop today? His situation is serious, whether or not he'll be released from the unfairly framed accusation, but why are you not praying?*

It was an important day in court because Bishop, who is the protective covering of our church and senior pastor of a big church in another state, would stand in court because he was wrongfully accused. No matter how busy I was, I had to intercede for him. It was an urgent situation where he could go to jail if anything went wrong. I promised to fast all day and intercede, but I had completely forgotten because of my grandchildren's problem.

When I looked at the clock, it was his scheduled time in court. Suddenly, I became alert and felt deep sorrow. Even then, my heart was still all over the place and I could not fully concentrate to intercede for Bishop. Because Bishop and the children filled my mind, it was extremely difficult to pray. I forced my soundless voice to start praying in tongues. For thirty minutes, I continued to pray, and I asked the Holy Spirit in my mind, "Please, help me." Slowly, I began to enter the presence of God, and the fear and anxiety that gripped my heart began to disappear. Instead of seeing my grandchildren, I began to see Bishop's sad situation in court. Through watching that vision, I was able to do a focused travailing prayer for thirty more minutes.

A Miracle

While I was praying, a miracle happened. My son, Jody, knocked on the door begged me to come out. I came out immediately from the room to see what was going on. Jody said that he just received a call from Heathers' mother, saying she changed her mind, and was returning home. She told him, "The reason I wanted to take the children was to provide them with comfort. But a moment ago the thought came to me: 'What benefit would it be if I forced the children who didn't want to go with me? These kids had already suffered a lot, and I don't want to add more to that.'"

After Jody told me what she had said, he began to jump up and down like a little child with joy.

The moment I heard the news I said, "Oh my God, Hallelujah! Thank You, Jesus! Wow, you did it again Jesus!" Like my son, I began to jump up and down, like a child, saying, "Thank You, Jesus. Thank You, Jesus."

Later that day, I heard the good news about my Bishop was found innocent of all charges. What a wonderful God that we serve. His faithfulness to be praised forevermore.

CHAPTER 6

THE HOLY SPIRIT HELPS
OUR PRAYERS

Just as Jesus is the Mediator for us, the Holy Spirit is also the Mediator who relentlessly seeks for us. The Bible tells us that the Holy Spirit who indwells every believer also prays for us. The Holy Spirit knows God's will better than anyone else and He offers perfect intercession. Praying according to God's Will is a perfect prayer that can be definitely answered. Our prayers speedily ascend to our Father God because the Holy Spirit prays for God's will to be done in us. Consequently, if we pray without the help of the Holy Spirit, we cannot pray perfectly. In addition, if we do not have the help of the Holy Spirit, the Lord's great purpose and providence will not be manifested in our lives.

(Romans 8:26) "Likewise the Spirit also helps in our weaknesses. For we do not know what we should pray for as we ought, but the Spirit Himself makes intercession for us with groanings which cannot be uttered."

Holy Spirit Prays According to God's Will

(Romans 8:27) "Now He who searches the hearts knows what the mind of the Spirit is, because He makes intercession for the saints according to the will of God."

The Bible tells us that He (God) who searches our hearts knows the mind of Spirit. Sometimes when we pray, we express things in a way that we didn't intend to or say things that we regret later, but when the Holy Spirit prays for us, He prays perfectly. For example, we might pray, "God, I hate this person; I wish he would vanish in front of my eyes." However, the Holy Spirit would never pray this way. When we pray in our heavenly language as we depend on the Holy Spirit, according to God's will the Spirit leads us to pray for forgiveness and pray to resist our anger. Moreover, He leads us to intercede for the one who disappointed us, gave us pain, and hurt us. When we have heartbreak, we want to completely express our pain but many times we cannot. Also, we want to scream out, cry out, and release all the anger that's inside of us, but many times we cannot do it. In these cases, we entrust ourselves to the Holy Spirit and pray in our heavenly language. Then He will help us restrain, forgive and our prayers reach God, because He does what we can't do on behalf of us; He leads us to pray perfectly according to God's will.

The Holy Spirit Leads Us to the Truth

When we pray in our heavenly language, the Holy Spirit can help us to realize our sin. In doing so, we can sincerely repent.

When I first believed in Jesus, I received Him as my Savior, but I didn't realize that I was a sinner. I thought I was a sinner because I didn't attend church. So I told God, "I'm sorry for not living the way You want me to. Please help me to go to church." I thought praying in this way would wash away all my sins. I also thought this was the way of serving God. I didn't know the truth, that if I believed in my heart and confessed Jesus with my mouth, I would be saved (Romans 10:9-10). I didn't know that if I confessed my sins, then He is faithful to cleanse me from all my unrighteousness (1John 1:9). I thought serving God meant attending church and giving offerings without skipping. But after I received the baptism of the Holy Spirit and prayed in my heavenly language, I came to an understanding that repentance without a personal encounter and relationship with God is meaningless.

Entrusting Myself Completely to the Holy Spirit

Oftentimes, when someone asks us to pray for them, we say, "Okay, I will pray." Then we do so with a ritualistic and formal prayer. What is prayer that is driven by the Holy Spirit? During our prayer, sometimes the Holy Spirit leads us to enter into the next level of prayer. That prayer comes from God's heart, follows God's voice, and prays according to what He desires. In the beginning, we start praying in our heavenly language by our own will. As we continue to pray, there's a moment where the Holy Spirit grips us. However, in many cases, we start the prayer, but because we aren't willing to wait until that "Holy Spirit" moment we give up too soon. As intercessors, we must press through by faith into God's presence so that we don't miss the moment of the Holy Spirit's inspiration and influence. So, we give up before we could experience God.

Testimony: Ritualistic and Formal Prayer

After I was spiritually born again, I prayed every day to God by reading my prayer list line by line; I had so many prayer topics after many years had passed. Then one day, as I was earnestly praying with my own words in my usual method, with my eyes closed, I vividly saw Pastor Kim's face, whom I had met a few times while I was in Korea a couple of years ago. Unexpectedly, and without any reason, I envisioned him with a sad countenance and tears running down his cheeks. I started to pray and cry out for Pastor Kim as emotion overtook me. Afterwards, I finished praying through my list. Then I asked, "God, why did I see Pastor Kim's face so vividly before me during prayer? Have I lost my mind?"

The Lord gave a deep impression on my heart. He said, "Do not give a formal or ritualistic prayer, but pray what the Holy Spirit desires. Pray as the Holy Spirit moves you and don't pray a constrained, formal prayer."

Subsequently, God began to train me to pray in my heavenly language as the Holy Spirit moved me, to give my prayer time completely to Him and not to follow my prayer list. It's funny to think about it now, but when I tried to pray down the prayer list as I used to, unbelievable incidents happened to me. Suddenly, I was unable to see any of the prayer lists that I used to peek at during prayer. After this happened several times, I finally gave into the Holy Spirit completely and I prayed in my heavenly language as the Holy Spirit inspired me. It was incredibly marvelous and surprising to be led by the Holy Spirit to pray all around the United States and around the world for my spiritual children, my friends, my partners, or missionaries.

Many times, when I try to pray in Korean or English I get lost, but if I pray as led by the Holy Spirit in my heavenly language, He knows what I don't know, and leads me to pray for what others really need. After going around the world led by the Holy Spirit, my spirit was full of joy and happiness. Through multiple times of my prayer experiences like this, I was able to enter deep into the presence of the Lord without a time limit and being tied to the prayer time.

Absolute Answers to Prayers

It can be quite adventurous to lay down all my schedule and plans, entrust myself completely to the Holy Spirit, and to pray as I'm led by Him. It's not about making my own time schedule, making my own prayer request at the time I want, and to pray only the prayer topics that I want to pray, then end it there. The prayer completely consigned to the Holy Spirit does not have a special or specific time; when the Holy Spirit ends, I also end. Therefore, I am assured that the prayer that is led by the Holy Spirit receives answers.

The reason is, through the joy and peace which comes to me after prayer, God gives me the faith that He's going to take care of the problems of the ones whom I am praying for.

For example, after praying for Pastor Kim, as led by the Holy Spirit, I found out later that he had gone on a short-term mission trip and was in a difficult situation because of an accident, and he desperately prayed to the Lord for help. Miraculously, he was able to safely return home. I'm sure the Holy Spirit impressed many intercessors to pray for Pastor Kim, but how many people obeyed the leading of the Holy Spirit? It may be my own thoughts but perhaps only a handful did.

Following the Guidance of the Holy Spirit

God's miracles manifest when someone intercedes for us. Through Christ who's in us, we can do all things in this world (Philippians 4:13). Although we may not have a relationship with unbelievers, we must pray for their redemption.

Sometimes when we pray, we may see a vision of a stranger's face. We should not ignore that person in that moment; instead follow the guidance of the Holy Spirit and pray for that person. Sometimes, a stranger's name pops up in our minds and we may receive a burden to pray for that person. At that moment pray, "Lord, I don't know this person, but with a heart of obedience I lift up this person to you. Thank you for using me as a praying tool for this person." Then pray in your heavenly language. You may not know anything about this person, but tears may flow, or a fullness of joy may come as if something started to happen.

God wants us to pray every time as we receive the Holy Spirit's inspiration. We may pray for someone we don't know but surprisingly we can experience the resolution of our own problem that was troubling us for a long time. God never receives anything without giving back. Whatever we offer Him, we can't imagine how He's going to reward us.

Testimony: A Dentist Visiting His Daughter

I fly frequently and spend many hours in an airplane. There is always someone whom I've never encountered before who sits next to me. I begin to intercede for this person, and whatever I sense the circumstance they are in, I always pray in my heavenly language as the Holy Spirit guides me. At times, God shows me a vision of them during or after praying. Sometimes He shows me their hard situations or family problems, and He tells me to quietly intercede. In some cases, God tells me to share the vision with the person, and what He is saying about it.

There have been many episodes, but there was one unforgettable encounter with a dentist who was going through a divorce. While I was praying for this man whom I've never met before and was seated next to me, suddenly, I saw a clear vision of a little girl who seemed to be his daughter. It looked like she was desperately and eagerly waiting for someone.

With the guidance of the Holy Spirit, I spoke to him kindly. "Where are you heading? Perhaps are you going to see your beautiful daughter?"

As soon as I said these words, he was startled and said, "Oh! How did you know that? Right now, I'm heading to Texas to meet my daughter."

"Oh, really? Whenever I fly, I have a habit of interceding for the person sitting next to me. While praying for you, I saw a five- to-six-year-old beautiful little girl. It seemed like she was eagerly waiting for someone."

He teared up as he was listening to my words and said, "Yes, you are right, she's my beautiful daughter who's turning six this year. Right now, I'm living in another state. A few months ago, my wife and I separated and we're in the process of a divorce. We have one daughter, and my wife took her to her mother's house in Texas. I haven't seen her for a few months so I'm going there to see her."

I asked him, "Can I pray for you?"

He replied, "Huh? Sure, thank you."

Then I prayed for his family's reconciliation and redemption. With all my heart, I prayed for them sincerely. Soon he confessed as tears streamed down his face. When he was younger, he said he believed in God and went to church, but when he grew up and married, he distanced himself from the church. He said that he'll take this opportunity and promised to attend church again when he goes back home. Then he handed me his business card and asked me to visit him when I get a chance. His business card noted that he was a dentist. I haven't seen that person since that time on the plane. Because I interceded for this man with the Holy Spirit's guidance, my earnest hope is for God to give this family a miracle of uniting them as one; and through His grace, the whole family would receive salvation and live a worthy life that serves the kingdom of God forever.

CHAPTER 7

WHY INTERCESSORY
PRAYER IS NEEDED

We intercede not only for the seasonal calling and the preparation of the revival, but we also intercede for many specific reasons.

1. Because Jesus intercedes, we as the body must also do likewise

We are the members of His body and of His flesh (Ephesians 5:30). Therefore, we must follow the path that the Lord has taken. We must participate in His ministry, because we are the body of Christ. Since Jesus and the Holy Spirit are in the intercessory ministry, we must also be in this ministry on behalf of others. As we intercede with Christ in this way, our prayers can bear its fruit.

> *(2 Corinthians 5:18) "Now all things are of God, who has reconciled us to Himself through Jesus Christ, and has given us the ministry of reconciliation"*

2. Help the weak through intercessory prayer

In the world, the strong get stronger by taking advantage of the weak, and the rich get richer by taking advantage of the poor. For example, "payday" loans might help someone pay their bills, but there is often a higher interest rate to pay, and the end result can be the person taking out the loan ends up in more debt.

Intercessors help the weak through prayer. The Bible says, "let the weak say I am strong; let the poor say I am rich" (Joel 3:10). Intercessors speak out verses like this over those they are praying for, allowing God to do His work in their lives.

> *(Romans 15:1) "We then who are strong ought to bear with the scruples of the weak, and not to please ourselves."*

3. Intercessory prayer is our response to God's love

"God is love" (1 John 4:8). Interceding for God's beloved souls is one way of accepting and returning His love. Since everything is His and all souls are precious to God, He desires to bring all things back to Himself. Normally, we tend to judge and discriminate against people by saying, "This person doesn't believe in God and this person believes God." When we see people who murdered someone, do drugs, do bad things to others, trample on people, and hurt people, we normally think or say it, "That person deserves to die." It is very difficult for us to intercede for them because we have a preconceived notion that they don't deserve to be loved.

> *(Romans 5:8) "But God demonstrates His own love toward us, in that while we were still sinners, Christ died for us."*

Regardless of what we think of these people, the important point is that God loves them. John 3:16 tells us that *"God so love the world…"* God sees all things with love. His love reaches out to the lost people whom Satan has deceived. God loves them and we are called to love them too. We cannot be better than God. If God does, then we must do as well … and we can do it *"through Christ who gives us strength"* (Philippians 4:13).

When we obey God's will and follow Him, surely, we will see His work. We are able to forgive those whom we couldn't forgive with our own strength, and genuinely intercede for those who offended and hurt us. If we cannot pray for them with God's compassion, then who will pray for them?

As God's intercessors, we shouldn't look at the person, no matter the condition of the individual. First, we must think, *What is God's heart towards them?* and look at them through the eyes and heart of God. Today, God is speaking to the faithful intercessors, *"Though you might hate their sin, have mercy on them and ceaselessly pray for them."* I would add that we can never forget that we are all *"sinners saved by grace."*

We must realize Father God's heart for all His beloved people to return to Him and we must cooperate with Him for His will to be fulfilled. The role of an intercessor is to pray for the abandoned people and to lead them to God's loving arms. This is because intercession is motivated by loving the soul.

Ultimately, we can't claim that we are doing God's work well, if we are not interceding for dying souls, and for the Church, the Body of Christ. Building the Church, missions, ministry, and every work of God is founded on intercessory prayer. We can't accomplish anything if we say that we are doing God's work, yet we are not interceding for our neighbors and the Church. Even the first church started with prayer (see Acts 2). They ordained missionaries and also prayed for them to send them to their mission fields (example, Acts 13:2). If we are not interceding for the lost, and God's people and kingdom, then how can we raise up the new church, experience miracles in our lives, or give God the glory?

4. Intercession is the fruit of loving the brothers and sisters

One of the reasons we intercede is that if we are part of God's family, then all of God's children are our sisters and brothers; it is only natural for us to pray for our spiritually-related sisters and brothers. We don't love reluctantly just because He has commanded us to love; we love because God's core character is love, and we imitate Him by loving our brothers and sisters in Christ (1 John 4:12, 16). If we don't love our sisters and brothers, we must ask ourselves if God is truly our Father. Loving the brethren means that I've acknowledged God as my Father, and hating my brother means that I'm not receiving God as my Father and rejecting Him.

The fruit of God's love is that we have received salvation. Just as giving birth to a child is the fruit of the parents, praying for another is also the fruit of love and its evidence. If we love our brothers and sisters, then we can powerfully intercede for them. Praying for someone without love only turns into formal, religious, and powerless people-pleasing prayer. Without love for the brothers in the intercessor's heart, we cannot rightly intercede for another according to God's desire. Through intercessory prayer, we can serve our sisters and brothers, serve our neighbors, and serve our nation. Intercessory prayer is a prayer of love for God and our neighbor. Ultimately, we cannot intercede without loving God and our brothers. It is joyful and rewarding for sincere Christians in sacrificing their time and body to pray for others. And God surely rewards them. Their life is destined to be radiant and fulfilled.

> *(1John 4:20) "If someone says, 'I love God,' and hates his brother, he is a liar; for he who does not love his brother whom he has seen, how can he love God whom he has not seen?"*

Is there anyone who prays, "God, punish this person!" because they hate that individual? Of course, when we get mad, we might show our anger and complain about that person. However, it's not easy to curse when we're praying. If we did pray in that manner, would God listen to our prayers? Most likely, it will not happen. Also, with the heart of hatred, will we be able to give a sincere blessing prayer towards them? In order to truly taste the fruit of prayer, we have to love our brothers and genuinely intercede for them: "God bless these people!"

5. Intercession prayer looks at the soul with compassion

(Matthew 14:14) "And when Jesus went out He saw a great multitude; and He was moved with compassion for them, and healed their sick."

Our Lord sees mankind with compassion. In Hebrew, compassion means, "Just as the mother's womb protects the sac of the baby; to embrace and protect another life." Cherishing and embracing another's life as our own means that we are embraced in the Lord's arms, and we are always safe in His mercy and love. When compassion enters our hearts, we are able to embrace another. Just as the Lord had compassion on the people in His society and loved them, we must also follow His example so that God's salvation can be accomplished through our intercessory prayer.

6. Intercessory prayer is a path of loving your enemy

(Matthew 5:44) "But I say to you, love your enemies, bless those who curse you, do good to those who hate you, and pray for those who spitefully use you and persecute you."

(Luke 6:27-28) "But I say to you who hear: Love your enemies, do good to those who hate you, bless those who curse you, and pray for those who spitefully use you."

The Bible shows that the Lord commanded us to love our enemies. Honestly, it is human nature to *not* pray for those who hurt us; we don't want our enemies to do well. So many times, His commands seem like a punishment to us. However, God leads us to a better way for our own sake, because loving the enemy is more beneficial to us than anybody else. When we are blessing someone, that blessing falls upon us as well. But when we are hating or cursing someone, that wave of hatred and curse falls upon us, too. The heart of unforgiveness and hatred toward the enemy eventually poisons us—and everyone around us (Hebrews 12:15).

God doesn't want us to hold onto hurt, which is why He taught us how to forgive. If there's a root of unforgiveness within us, we can never stand in the gap and fulfill the calling of a mediator. For the intercessor, it is not an option but a requirement to forgive. Forgiving our enemies is an opportunity for us to pull out the whole root of the Devil's work. But it is extremely difficult for us to forgive with our own strength. However, It is also impossible to love our enemy, show kindness to them, and bless them with our own human strength. Therefore, we must seek God as to how this person harmed us and what led them to do so. In that moment of hurt, we invite Jesus into that situation, so that we can receive inner healing. Only then true forgiveness is possible.

First, we have to see the problem within us and realize and understand where this scar came from. This can give us compassion, and then we can intercede for our enemy. We are allowing him to bind us. Hating someone is like inviting the Devil into our lives. We are allowing the Devil to bind us. The Devil will destroy us first before he destroys our offender. We must refuse the Devil from entering our mind. Once the Devil has an open door into our lives, the forces of evil will dominate our hearts and slowly extinguish the work of the Holy Spirit, and the inspiration of the Holy Spirit can't manifest. Therefore, we cannot pray according to God's will and live in His will, which can eventually destroy us.

When we are not harboring hatred towards another, we can offer an impartial intercessory prayer that God desires. Taking the action of loving the offender eradicates the Devil work. Loving the offender is like spiritually "sweeping and cleaning the house" that the Devil has built within us. We throw out all the spiritual garbage through forgiveness, repentance, and blessing others. If the entire root of bitterness is removed and our hearts are clean, then surprisingly it will be completely filled with God's love. When we are emotionally healed, we can experience God's love and it releases the work of blessing, which will allow us to offer a powerful intercessory prayer for our brothers. We will see our prayers being answered, and our faith will grow daily. If we were to fully understand the "royal law of love" (James 2:8), then we can offer intercessory prayers of blessing to our offender, and we will experience God's overflowing grace.

CHAPTER 8

TESTIMONY:
MY MINISTRY IN KOREA THAT OPENED
AFTER 30 YEARS OF LIVING IN THE
UNITED STATES

My fasting prayer book, *If My People* was first published in 1992 in America (it will soon be revised and republished) and was translated and published in Korean with the title of *Inner-Healing Through Prayer* in 2001. In 1987, my first book of testimony, *Bad Luck Baby* was published in America (it will also soon be revised and republished), and was translated in Korean as *Bad Luck Baby* in 2002, through the Bethany publishing company. Through the advertisement and rental of the Christian Hall from the publishing company, I was given the opportunity to share my testimony in front of many pastors, laymen, and spiritually hungry Christians whom I've never met before.

Soon after, people from Korea who had read my book and were touched and received grace, surprisingly called me, asking that I come and teach them inner-healing and intercessory prayer. I was living a busy life, and felt like I needed more than ten bodies; I was pastoring with my late husband, and I often traveled throughout the states, and out of the country through Sunshine Ministries. But no matter how busy I was, I couldn't reject the request I received from Korea.

For the first time in 30 years since I came to the U.S., my name, Sun Fannin (Korean name: Sun Tok Chong) was recognized in Korea through my testimony book. I will never forget the book cover. Above the title *Bad Luck Baby* were the words, "From the miserable, messy life to an authority of inner healing." Yes, that is right. My life in Korea was absolutely at the bottom. But I was saved by the unconditional grace of God and became a new person, and I had so much to say to people in Korea. I wanted to share that, "I didn't know Jesus back then, so I lived under the curse of being a bad luck baby in Korea. But after meeting Jesus in America, I became a new person!"

Expansion of the Seminar in Korea

Splitting my busy schedule, I often went to Korea and gathered intercessors to teach them the power of intercessory prayer and restoration through inner healing. The vision that God gave me was to first teach these people to be emotionally healed and restored, then to become effective intercessors. I then taught these people how to intercede and to perform inner healing prayer ministry.

I created all the teaching materials and freely shared everything, so they could re-teach the same material at places I could not go to, and show the love of Jesus to those who needed healing, restoration, and prayer. The news spread from one person to another, and as people were introduced to intercessory prayer, my inner-healing and restoration seminar was expanded. Before the seminar, I mainly focused on discipleship training for lay people to become ministers, because I believed that was the calling and mission God gave me to help build local churches. But one day, surprisingly, several pastors and lay ministers visited me because they were interested in intercessory prayer, inner-healing, and restoration.

Starting a New Work

I had never planned for this, but a few pastors and lay ministers wanted to attend the inner healing and restoration seminar, which normally only regular church members attended. So, I started a new work, a restoration seminar for pastors and lay ministers. At that time, my ministry schedule in Korea was always tight and I didn't have enough time to minister to everyone. However, God made it possible for pastors and lay ministers to attend my meetings, so they could then teach their congregations. It was definitely a better plan than mine. God already knew and planned what I could never have imagined!

Wherever the Lord Calls

By the grace of God, the news spread gradually all over Korea that I had come from America to teach intercessory prayer and restoration ministry in Korea. I was invited to inner healing seminars and also was requested to hold intercessory prayer conferences at many churches. I gave as much as I could, but there was a limit to my time. Although I may have been dehydrated and was to the point of fainting, my calling from God was so precious, I ran relentlessly straight towards where He was calling me. As a result, there was an overflowing grace of God whenever and wherever I traveled.

CHAPTER 9

HOW TO INTERCEDE

We can learn the specific steps of intercession through the Word of God.

1. Spiritual Warfare

Intercessory prayer is spiritual warfare. We must go into spiritual warfare in order to see the work of healing and salvation. God's will is to shine His salvation and glory on all people. But the Devil distracts people from fulfilling God's will in their lives, and interferes with God's people helping others, especially if they are expanding God's kingdom. Then the Devil actively hinders and causes them to become despondent towards God through disappointment and frustration. This is why intercessors are essential in helping unbelievers to believe. Therefore, through intercessory prayer, we must guide them to the Lord.

> *(2 Corinthians 4:4) "Whose minds the god of this age has blinded, who do not believe, lest the light of the gospel of the glory of Christ, who is the image of God, should shine on them."*

We must wage war in spiritual battle through intercessory prayer for the souls who are "blinded by the god of this age" and can't see the light of the gospel of Christ (2 Corinthians 4:4). When we do spiritual warfare through intercessory prayer, the unsaved and the backslidden can be touched and transformed by the Holy Spirit. Therefore, praying for the salvation of others is fighting with travails and tears, and requires much patience. Oftentimes, we get discouraged when we don't get God's answers quickly. However, when we enter His presence as we engage in spiritual warfare against the spirit of darkness, we can eventually see and obtain all that's available from God. It might take some time, so we must fight and cast out any evil spirit hindering us from entering His presence.

The strongholds that most often block us from encountering the Lord are disappointment and discouragement, hatred and anger, pride and arrogance, greed and gluttony, worry and concern, fear and anxiety, adultery and lust, stubbornness and disobedience. It is only when we destroy these strongholds through spiritual battle that we can encounter Him. Intercessory prayer is possible only when we fight spiritual warfare in the name of Jesus. The Devil won't flee when we come with a timid attitude and say, "Please leave me alone." He would rather accuse and mock us (see John 10:10; Revelations 12:10). We must have quick discernment and cast out all evil spirits that want to swallow us up.

For example, God already gave Daniel the answer on his first day of fasting, but because of the spiritual warfare against the spirit of darkness that had taken control over the air, it took 21 days to receive God's response.

(Daniel 10:12-14) "Then he said to me, 'Do not fear, Daniel, for from the first day that you set your heart to understand, and to humble yourself before your God, your words were heard; and I have come because of your words. But the prince of the kingdom of Persia withstood me twenty-one days; and behold, Michael, one of the chief princes, came to help me, for I had been left alone there with the kings of Persia. Now I have come to make you understand what will happen to your people in the latter days, for the vision refers to many days yet to come.'"

Angels have different ranks, and they care for us according to their given positions. The Devil's army has different ranks too. We must pray to attack and dominate each area where evil spirits have taken root. Back in the olden days, Koreans used to believe there were gods for each mountain.

Each village had their own god, and whenever the church was established in the village the evil spirits didn't leave quietly.

When we engage in spiritual warfare, we must discern which spirit we are fighting. Whenever we start something new in God's work, one thing we must remind ourselves is that we are definitely going to be attacked spiritually. If we know the enemy's tactics in advance and are equipped with prayer, then we can avoid his schemes and can have victory in our spiritual battle (2 Corinthians 2:11).

When Adam sinned, all the authority of the world was forfeited and passed to the Devil.

> *(Luke 4:6) "And the devil said to Him, 'All this authority I will give You, and their glory; for this has been delivered to me, and I give it to whomever I wish.'"*

When Jesus came, died on the cross and resurrected after three days. He restored the power that was usurped by the Devil. The enemy has stolen our peace, joy, reconciliation, love, healing, health, finances, family, etc. and we must retrieve it in the name of Jesus Christ.

A. The Spiritual Weapons We Use in Spiritual Warfare

> *(Hosea 4:6) "My people are destroyed for lack of knowledge. Because you have rejected knowledge, I also will reject you from being priest for Me; Because you have forgotten the law of your God, I also will forget your children."*

The cause of many of the problems that we face is due to our lack of rightly understanding God's ways. We overcome by the Word of God, the blood of the Lamb, and the word of our testimony; otherwise, we will face more tests, tribulations and difficulties (Revelation 12:11). When we face these kinds of problems, intercessors must discern how the Devil is causing us to fail. It is important to know why, because he distracts our prayers and affects us from making the right judgments by causing us to be frustrated and confused when we face difficult situations.

In these end times, spiritual warfare is becoming more aggressive. God wants us to know His strategies and know how to use them. He wants intercessors to win the spiritual warfare against the spirit of darkness that's set up today on this earth.

> *(2 Corinthians 10:4-5) "For the weapons of our warfare are not carnal but mighty in God for pulling down strongholds, casting down arguments and every high thing that exalts itself against the knowledge of God, bringing every thought into captivity to the obedience of Christ"*

As intercessors engage in spiritual warfare against evil spirits, we need suitable weapons. We do not use man-made weapons such as missiles or guns, but spiritual weapons to go against the evil spirits. Only God-given weapons can crush the power of the enemy. Many intercessors expect to be liberated from their own difficult circumstances, yet they hesitate to pay the price. The price is to acknowledge and obey that God is the Lord in all areas of our lives. Spiritual weapons include prayer, the Word of God, obedience, faith, trust, praise, worship, spiritual gifts, and many others. Above all, the strongest and most effective weapon is *humility*. As the intercessor comes before God in humility and prays for others, we will see the fruit of our prayers.

> *(1 Peter 5:6) "Therefore humble yourselves under the mighty hand of God, that He may exalt you in due time."*

Humility is the place we stand before God when the enemy comes against us.

B. The Most Foundational Spiritual Warfare

Our spiritual weapons become ineffective when we give the Devil a foothold and open a spiritual door.

> *(Ephesians 4:27) "Do not give the devil a foothold."*

In the Greek language, the word "foothold" means, "to give any opportunity, environment, door and place to the devil." Evil spirits cannot live in the light because they are eternally trapped in darkness by God.

> *(John 3:19-21) "And this is the condemnation, that the light has come into the world, and men loved darkness rather than light, because their deeds were evil. <u>For everyone practicing evil hates the light and does not come to the light, lest his deeds should be exposed.</u> But he who does the truth comes to the light, that his deeds may be clearly seen, that they have been done in God"* (emphasis, mine).

Permitting the realm of darkness within us means that we are opening the door for evil spirits to work in that realm. Intercessors must learn the method of defeating the Devil. He has been successful in deceiving mankind for thousands of years; hence he knows how to deceive us very well. People tend to believe the Devil's lies more than God's Word. Intercessors must not agree with these lies, such as the whispers that we *can't* do all things through Christ who gives us strength (Philippians 4:13).

> *(James 4:7) "Therefore submit to God. Resist the devil and he will flee from you."*

First and foremost, intercessors must have an attitude of obedience to God's will and the Word of God in our lives, in order to resist the Devil. The more we invest our time in seeking the face of the Lord, and the more we give our lives over to the Word of God, we will become more confident in dealing with the temptations and doubts that come our way.

When Jesus was in the wilderness for 40 days, the Devil used God's Word to tempt Him. But Jesus used the Word to oppose him.

> *(Matthew 4:4) "But He answered and said, 'It is written, 'Man shall not live by bread alone, but by every word that proceeds from the mouth of God.'"*

Intercessors can cast out evil spirits by believing and declaring the Word of God. When we obey the Word and resist the Devil and his cohorts, they flee from us. Obeying the Lord and believing in His Word is the way to banish the Devil and move towards God.

C. Satan's Greatest Weapon: Lies

> *(John 8:43-44) "Why do you not understand My speech? Because you are not able to listen to My word. You are of your father the devil, and the desires of your father you want to do. He was a murderer from the beginning, and does not stand in the truth, because there is no truth in him. When he speaks a lie, he speaks from his own resources, for he is a liar and the father of it."*

The reason why many intercessors are vulnerable and fail is because they've been deceived by the Devil's lies. Often, the Devil distorts God's Word of Truth to look like his lies.

> *(Romans 1:25) "Who exchanged the truth of God for the lie, and worshiped and served the creature rather than the Creator, who is blessed forever. Amen."*

If we don't know the Word of God, we will end up believing Satan's lies. When that happens, we will not experience God's blessings, we will be ignorant of the truth, and live a frustrating life. Through the Lord's prayer, Jesus taught His disciples not to fall into temptation and to be delivered from evil. It is absolutely biblical for intercessors to pray to not fall for the Devil's temptations and lies.

> *(Matthew 6:13) "And do not lead us into temptation but deliver us from the evil one. For Yours is the kingdom and the power and the glory forever. Amen."*

Jesus spoke again to His disciples on Gethsemane.

> *(Matthew 26:41) "Watch and pray, lest you enter into temptation. The spirit indeed is willing, but the flesh is weak."*

When Jesus was on earth, He exposed the Devil's lies and temptation and had victories by the power of faithful and continuous prayer. Since Jesus did as such, intercessors must also follow His example.

2. Praying in the Heavenly Language

> *(Acts 2:4) "And they were all filled with the Holy Spirit and began to speak with other tongues, as the Spirit gave them utterance."*

Based on their denomination, Christians have different opinions about praying in tongues and prayer led by the Holy Spirit. It has been my experience that praying in tongues aligns my prayers with the will of God. As well, there are times when I'm prompted by the Holy Spirit to pray over someone or a specific situation. At these times, I intercede as led by the Holy Spirit, and I often see or hear of answers to prayer in a very short time. As intercessors, we must pray in the Spirit (speaking in tongues) and pray with understanding (1 Corinthians 14:15).

Prayer led by the Holy Spirit is absolutely necessary because the Lord allows us to pray according to His will.

> *(Romans 8:26-27) "Likewise the Spirit also helps in our weaknesses. For we do not know what we should pray for as we ought, but the Spirit Himself makes intercession for us with groanings which cannot be uttered. Now He who searches the hearts knows what the mind of the Spirit is, because He makes intercession for the saints according to the will of God."*

The Lord is aware of our heart and spiritual condition. Oftentimes when we come before the Lord to pray, we are frustrated and don't know where to start because of life's burdens and the pressure we feel.

A Pastor's Testimony

I have never forgotten the message of a particular pastor's sermon. He said he always implores his congregation to pray in their heavenly language and he always prays in tongues before the congregation. The result of his ministry method sent his disciples to all parts of the world and established churches, and today his church has grown into a mega church. How could this pastor pray individually for all his congregation, for the churches of his disciples, and the missionaries spread all over the world? How would he know the needs of all these people?

Sometimes, he said he suffered and groaned countless days before the Lord because of the heavy pressure from the responsibility of running a large church. He said that with his own ability it was very difficult to lead a mega church with the vision of world evangelism. Numerous times, when he came before the Lord, he didn't even know how and what to pray. But he said whenever this happened, he was led by the Holy Spirit through praying in his heavenly language. Even though he said he couldn't pay attention to the smallest details, through the Holy Spirit, he was able to pray to cover all minor and major prayer topics. With the help of the Holy Spirit, he knew how and what to pray for his church and congregation and he received the wisdom to lead the great denomination. Although we may understand the specific importance of prayer, without the Holy Spirit we won't know exactly how to pray for ourselves and the souls of those around us.

A. Heavenly Prayer that Speaks Mysteries to God

(1 Corinthians 14:2) "For he who speaks in a tongue does not speak to men but to God, for no one understands him; however, in the spirit he speaks mysteries."

This verse shows us that heavenly prayer is not for men but to God. We can say that it is more effective to pray in our heavenly language than any spoken words that we communicate with Him. For example, if I tell a secret to someone, that person will keep the secret when we are in a good relationship, but when this relationship breaks down, that same person will most likely reveal the secret. However, we don't have to worry when we tell our secrets to God.

Sometimes when we pray in our heavenly language, we may not feel the depth or may feel unsatisfied. Then you are more likely to feel that you are praying in the wrong way. Again, the Devil will provoke and mock us to put a barrier between us and God. The Devil may whisper lies such as:

- "What are you muttering about?"
- "Your prayer is useless."
- "You really look like a crazy person."
- "You don't even know what you are saying, and you are wasting your time."

Oftentimes the Devil's deception causes us to stop praying in tongues. However, we need an active, engaging attitude to continuously persist in prayer without being deceived by the enemy's devices. The Devil is a liar. If he tries to distract us in our prayer, we must completely rebuke what he is saying.

B. The Power of the Holy Spirit

(Acts 1:8) "But you shall receive power when the Holy Spirit has come upon you; and you shall be witnesses to Me in Jerusalem, and in all Judea and Samaria, and to the end of the earth."

There are nine spiritual gifts including praying in tongues (1 Corinthians 12:4-10), and the evidence of being baptized in the Holy Spirit is speaking in tongues (Acts 2:4). All believers can speak in tongues, if they desire to do so by asking the Holy Spirit for this gift.

C. Praying in Tongues is for our Spiritual Growth

(1 Corinthians 14:4) "He who speaks in a tongue edifies himself, but he who prophesies edifies the church."

Edifying himself means making our spirit abundantly fruitful. By looking at one's appearance, we can't understand their inner condition. But the Holy Spirit, who examines our hearts, knows well of all the details of our heart. Through the Holy Spirit, our Lord Jesus knows all our hidden pain, scars, sins, and weaknesses, and he knows the person he created us to be. As we speak in tongues, it opens the way for the Holy Spirit to work. Therefore, the Holy Spirit intercedes for us according to our Father God's will.

(Jude 1:20) "But you, beloved, building yourselves up on your most holy faith, praying in the Holy Spirit."

(James 3:6) "And the tongue is a fire, a world of iniquity. The tongue is so set among our members that it defiles the whole body and sets on fire the course of nature; and it is set on fire by hell."

The tongue is the worldliest part of our body. If we speak in our heavenly language more frequently, we won't have time to speak negative or coarse words. As such, speaking in our heavenly language has many benefits.

D. Praying According to God's Will

> *(1John 5:14-15) "Now this is the confidence that we have in Him, that if we ask anything according to His will, He hears us. And if we know that He hears us, whatever we ask, we know that we have the petitions that we have asked of Him."*

This verse shows that the Lord has promised He will answer our prayers when we pray according to His will. When we pray in tongues, we are praying according to the will of the Lord. Praying in tongues is prayer led by the Holy Spirit, and the Holy Spirit knows the Lord's will better than we do. The Holy Spirit intercedes for us and through us. He wants to fulfill the will of the Lord. There is a limit to praying in our own language, but praying in tongues is limitless. We can pray on a deeper level through praying in tongues. We can receive a quick answer to our prayers if we pray in tongues by relying on the Holy Spirit. As the Bible tells us, God will work only when we pray according to His will. Pray in tongues if you want to know God's will about your marriage, or business, or any area of your life that you are unsure of.

E. The Importance of Praying in Tongues

> *(1Corinthians 14:18) "I thank my God I speak with tongues more than you all."*

Paul said to Corinthian church that he prayed in tongues more than all of them. Therefore, he overcame persecution and calamity, and as the person who wrote two thirds of the New Testament, he teaches us the truth of God's grace and His laws. Intercessors must pray in tongues much more than they pray in their natural language. In my case, there were many times my late husband woke me up because I prayed in tongues even in my sleep. Praying in tongues has become a habit in my life. Pastor Larry used to joke to members of our church that we sleep in separate rooms because I speak in tongues during the night and I wake him up.

F. Pray in the Spirit, Worship in the Spirit

(1 Corinthians 14:14-18) "For if I pray in a tongue, my spirit prays, but my understanding is unfruitful. What is the conclusion then? I will pray with the spirit, and I will also pray with the understanding. I will sing with the spirit, and I will also sing with the understanding. Otherwise, if you bless with the spirit, how will he who occupies the place of the uninformed say 'Amen' at your giving of thanks, since he does not understand what you say? For you indeed give thanks well, but the other is not edified. I thank my God I speak with tongues more than you all."

As our faith grows, we must trust in the Lord, pray and worship in the Spirit, and overcome doubt and fear.

G. Pray in the Spirit at All Times

(Ephesians 6:18) "Praying always with all prayer and supplication in the Spirit, being watchful to this end with all perseverance and supplication for all the saints."

How does the heavenly language fall upon us? There are times that people pray in tongues simply by having a fellow believer lay hands on them, and sometimes they receive this gift independently, with the Holy Spirit resting on them. The important key is that we must begin with faith. Show your faith by your actions. There are instances when the Holy Spirit comes upon us suddenly, but it is uncommon. First, we must start with our own will and faith. It may seem like a trivial matter, but God will guide us delicately once we obey Him.

3. Travailing Prayer

The dictionary definition of travailing is, "strenuous mental or physical effort, grief, pain, tumult and child-bearing toil." In Hebrew, it means suffering and pain.

The travailing experience during prayer is a different level that originates from the inner man. Travailing prayer can be compared to a woman conceiving and giving birth to a child. Life is brought on this earth through the pain of pregnancy and labor. Similarly, God also has travailing pain to raise the church on this earth for His holy Kingdom.

Through our fellowship with God in His Word and prayer, He plants in us the seed of His will and plan. Through those seeds planted in us, He brings to pass His will and plans on this earth.

As the woman uses all her strength to give birth to a child, the spiritual person also uses strength for God's will to be done in travailing prayer.

It is like the Holy Spirit pushing out the life of the Spirit to be born in the midst of the travailing prayer and lamentation. Unless the mother uses her strength to push the child, the child cannot be born. It goes the same with the spiritual world.

In order to bring God's will to pass for ourselves and our neighbors, whom we are interceding, we need the same effort, toil, and pain of travailing.

Just like a mother goes through travailing when giving birth, we also go through travailing prayer when breaking down the spiritual stronghold and destroying the Devil's plans.

A. Travailing Prayer of Elijah

Elijah, endured through travailing prayer for the rain to fall on Israel's land. He prays the same prayer seven times to bring rain down. The image of Elijah praying is the same way in which a woman gives birth. Instead of praying once or twice and being exhausted, saying, "This is enough!" he continuously prayed intensely seven times. Finally, it rained in answer to his prayer. When you endure any sacrifice and pray, the heavens will open and the fruit that God wants to give will be poured out. The result of our prayer depends on how much we sacrifice and the level of our desperation.

> *(1 Kings 18:42-44) "So Ahab went up to eat and drink. And Elijah went up to the top of Carmel; then he bowed down on the ground, and put his face between his knees, and said to his servant, 'Go up now, look toward the sea.' So, he went up and looked, and said, 'There is nothing.' And seven times he said, 'Go again.' Then it came to pass the seventh time, that he said, 'There is a cloud, as small as a man's hand, rising out of the sea!' So he said, 'Go up, say to Ahab, 'Prepare your chariot, and go down before the rain stops you."*

B. Travailing Prayer Is Powerful Weapon

A travailing prayer is a powerful weapon in the Holy Spirit. It is giving birth to God's vision and His will that's planted in us.

> *(Isaiah 42:13-14) "The LORD shall go forth like a mighty man; He shall stir up His zeal like a man of war. He shall cry out, yes, shout aloud; He shall prevail against His enemies. LORD 'I have held My peace a long time, I have been still and restrained Myself. Now I will cry like a woman in labor, I will pant and gasp at once.'"*

This verse shows that we are to cry out before God in travailing prayer, like a woman in labor. Born again Christians are readied instruments for the indwelling Holy Spirit to travail in spiritual lamentation, toil, and groaning. If Christians desire to be used in this way, then the Holy Spirit will reveal the spiritual reality through their prayer.

(Isaiah 66:8) "Who has heard such a thing? Who has seen such things? Shall the earth be made to give birth in one day? Or shall a nation be born at once? For as soon as Zion was in labor, she gave birth to her children."

C. Travailing Prayer Embraces Another Soul

Intercessory prayer is the work of embracing another soul and giving birth to new life within them. It is embracing another in our heart and travailing for them. When we embrace another person in our hearts, their soul can then be transformed. For example, the person interceding for healing must hold the Lord with one hand and deliver God's healing power to be transferred to the one who's in need of healing. Just like a pregnant woman, we must carry the power of the Lord's healing, then give birth to that healing. You must surrender your life for God's power to work through you for your loved ones to be healed.

When we begin to feel the desperation of suffering people to be restored, we must give birth to healing by either crying out or by expressing our thoughts, offering all our sweat and strength. In that very moment, we are used as God's womb. The Lord wants us to be vessels that can bear the power of the Lord and give birth to it. Those interceding for the one who's travailing is like a midwife who helps a pregnant woman give birth. The representative travailing in prayer thinks about only one thing: "I want all these people to be healed. I earnestly want it. I'm desperate. I want God's healing power to be manifest upon them. I want to see a miracle right now." At times, intercessors may experience the same pain of suffering in our hearts or physical pain in our bodies as those we are praying for.

D. Travailing Prayer Is Momentary Pain and Everlasting Joy

When God answers our prayer after travailing, we forget all the hardships we've experienced. No matter how painful during prayer, we forget all the hardships and are grateful when we see the results. Through enduring travailing prayer in intercession, a greater level of evangelism becomes possible. We can also experience a quick answer to our prayers. There must be the Word of God, faith, and intercessory prayer within the church and people who are evangelizing.

> *(John 16:20-21) "Most assuredly, I say to you that you will weep and lament, but the world will rejoice; and you will be sorrowful, but your sorrow will be turned into joy. A woman, when she is in labor, has sorrow because her hour has come; but as soon as she has given birth to the child, she no longer remembers the anguish, for joy that a human being has been born into the world."*

> *(Hebrews 5:7) "Who [Jesus], in the days of His flesh, when He had offered up prayers and supplications, with vehement cries and tears to Him who was able to save Him from death, and was heard because of His godly fear."*

E. Travailing Prayer Is the Holy Spirit's Tool

Today, God is looking for intercessors who are willing to be an instrument of the Holy spirit to offer travailing prayer to birth God's work on this earth. God is ready to birth out the spiritual revival and His will to be done. But what about us? Are we ready? If we become intercessors, offering travailing prayer as an instrument of the Holy Spirit, we can experience a spiritual revival in our nation, city, church, and economy. We can also witness people's lives changed by the power of God.

Through the Holy Spirit, God sows the dream, calling, and vision for the revival of our church and nation in our lives. This is why we have to be spiritually alive in prayer. God never stops what He has begun (Philippians 1:6). God never aborts His spiritual children but gave birth to them. However, when churches cease to pray, God's people will miss out on His transformation of their lives.

F. Real Pain and Fake Pain

When giving birth to a baby, there is temporary pain that is not the real pain. When we are interceding, we may feel like, "This is it!" but if we are not seeing actual transformation then we must go back to praying again. Just as we must wait patiently until a baby is birthed, transformation will happen when we wait patiently for the person to change. If we claim that we are intercessors with our lips, yet we can't endure for that one soul and don't have the heart to sacrifice for that one, then we don't have the right to be called an intercessor.

The Vision God Gave for Our Church

The vision God gave to our church from the beginning until now is "love, acceptance, and forgiveness." When I first received this vision, I was deeply touched. However, from the moment I received it, all kinds of difficulties began. The abandoned people in this world, people who do strange things, people who were in and out of prison, people who were addicted to drugs and alcohol, and even people who have been married many times were the types of people who came to our church. I was stunned and thought this was absurd. "Oh God, what do you want me to do with these people?"

I thought I was the only one who had problems, but compared to them, my problems were nothing. For example, why do some people lie so much? In order to do drugs, they would lie that they don't have anything to eat. When we gave them money to buy food, they would use it to buy drugs instead. After hearing all kinds of lies, I couldn't tell if they were hungry or if they were going to use the money for drugs. Then God spoke to me: *"Love them, forgive them, and accept them."* Strangely, if I kept myself apart from these people, I was unable to truly intercede for them. Only formal and ritualistic prayer came out of my mouth.

Embracing Unconditionally

Then one day God touched me by saying, *"If you don't embrace each of these souls individually, they will not be transformed."* From that moment on, I started to pray in the Holy Spirit for each person. As I cried and prayed, "God, I feel the same pain as if my stomach was tearing when giving birth to a baby." I cried in travailing prayer in the upper room and again at church. When I met each person, I hugged them unconditionally and said, "God loves you. God doesn't judge you." I embraced each person with tears and didn't care about their terrible smell. When I did so, at some point I couldn't even smell them anymore, and I didn't reject them even when they did something I would hate.

The Beginning of Transformation

As time went by, these people were set free from alcohol and drug addiction. And those who were depressed and living in hopelessness after a divorce began to change and live a joyful Christian life in a new found hope. Our church didn't have an official morning prayer and this was usually when I met with God, but somehow, one by one, they began to find out and gathered with me. These people who previously were only focused on themselves came to join me in intercessory prayer. Finally, the fire of revival began to flame.

Our church's unique strength is that there are many who have been with us since the beginning of our church. Today, they are very zealous in prayer as intercessors.

The Intercessory Prayer of Moses

Moses earnestly interceded for the forgiveness of the people by risking his name and life.

> *(Exodus 32:32) "Yet now, if You will forgive their sin but if not, I pray, blot me out of Your book which You have written."*

The Intercessory Prayer of Paul

Apostle Paul loved his people to the extent that he interceded for them, even if it would cause him to be accursed and cut off from Christ.

> *(Romans 9:1-3) "I tell the truth in Christ, I am not lying, my conscience also bearing me witness in the Holy Spirit, that I have great sorrow and continual grief in my heart. For I could wish that I myself were accursed from Christ for my brethren, my countrymen according to the flesh."*

Latter Rain for the Last Harvest

> *(Zechariah 10:1) "Ask the Lord for rain in the time of the latter rain. The Lord will make flashing clouds; He will give them showers of rain, grass in the field for everyone."*

> *(James 5:7) "Therefore be patient, brethren, until the coming of the Lord. See how the farmer waits for the precious fruit of the earth, waiting patiently for it until it receives the early and latter rain."*

The farmer waits for the fruit to ripe but without rain he can't reap the harvest. There must be a later rain in order to reap the last harvest. The "rain" is representative of intercessory prayer.

Souls must be spiritually thirsty for spiritual rain to come, just as the dry land is waiting for the rain to come. In order to see the latter rain with God's miraculous work, travailing prayer is absolutely necessary.

> *(James 5:17-18) "Elijah was a man with a nature like ours, and he prayed earnestly that it would not rain; and it did not rain on the land for three years and six months. And he prayed again, and the heaven gave rain, and the earth produced its fruit."*

CHAPTER 10

THE POWER OF INTERCESSORY PRAYER TESTIMONIES: THE BEGINNING OF DISCIPLESHIP IN CALIFORNIA

Spiritual Breakthrough #1

The Korean Church in Oakland, California

In March 2003, I was invited as a guest speaker to a conference at a Korean Church in Oakland, California. I had attended and ministered at mainly American church seminars and conferences for about 20 years, so I was a bit uncomfortable and unfamiliar with speaking in a Korean-American church. As well, ever since God opened my ministry in Korea two years ago, I have lived a busy life due to traveling back and forth. I used this as an excuse to refuse the invitation, whenever I was asked to speak at Korean churches in the U.S.

Then one day, the Holy Spirit touched me: *"Open your heart about going to the Korean Church in America."*

I replied, "Yes God, I'll go as You open the door." I received His words with an obedient heart, I gladly accepted the invitation to speak at the Korean church in California.

Every March, I go to Korea and Japan for two weeks; but this time, instead of coming straight home to Indiana after this trip, I planned on attending the three-day conference in California.

Losing My Handbag

After ministry in Korea was over, I arrived at Incheon Airport, got my ticket, and checked in my bags to head back to America. To have a little more fellowship before leaving, I sat down in a quiet area in the airport with two pastors from Korea who came to say good-bye, along with a pastor from Northern California who was flying back with me. After much laughter and a joyful time of sharing, I got ready to enter the gate only to find that the handbag that I placed next to me was missing. I would not have seen someone swiftly grabbing my bag as they passed by, because I was so focused on our conversation.

I was so shocked as I looked around everywhere for my handbag, but it was gone. It felt as though the whole world was collapsing. In my handbag was the offering money from the two weeks of ministry in Japan and Korea, my driver license, and two Visa cards for emergencies. Worst of all, I had my airplane ticket and my passport in the handbag. I could call my husband to cancel the Visa cards, and the driver license could be reissued when I arrived home, but without the ticket and passport, flying back to the U.S. was impossible. My mind went blank. "Oh Lord!" I repeated as I paced the floor nervously and searched for an airport security guard. Unfortunately, we were sitting in the area where there was no CCTV, so they couldn't find any evidence of someone taking my handbag.

Spiritual War Has Begun

Losing my handbag and its contents was heartbreaking, but I felt even worse that I could no longer attend the seminar in Oakland, because the congregation had been praying and waiting for months.

All of a sudden, a thought came to contact my home in the U.S. to tell them of the situation, and to request intercessory prayer. As soon as my husband received my call, he urgently emailed our church's intercessors. Also, when the Oakland church heard my news, they began to engage in spiritual warfare and interceded relentlessly. While heading to the U.S. embassy from the airport, the pastors and I continued our spiritual warfare, and in the name of Jesus we opposed, destroyed, crushed, and demolished the Devil's evil plan of stopping me from going to the seminar in the Korean church.

A Miracle of God

I was so thankful to have the pastors who drove me urgently to the U.S. embassy, and I kept muttering to myself, "Thank you, Lord. Thank you, Lord." While in this difficult circumstance, I continued to offer God a thanksgiving prayer, and by the time we arrived at the U.S. Embassy it was already 3 p.m. In the lobby, there were a few people who had an appointment, and there were others like me who came in because of an urgent situation for an interview. We all waited for our names to be called.

Despite knowing that I should wait, I was so anxious and impatient that I approached the teller and called the staff inside and told my whole story. Graciously, they set a time for me to meet the Consul in person. A few minutes later, the Consul came to the lobby, called my name, and motioned me to come inside. Though he heard some parts of the story from the staff, he kindly asked me to talk about my situation in detail. When I finished, the Consul made a temporary passport and, on the spot, he handed me $50 saying that I shouldn't enter the U.S. without a penny. He even shook my hands with warmth and love as he blessed me with God's protection. After receiving the temporary passport, we continued to do spiritual warfare by speaking in our heavenly language over the busy traffic in downtown Seoul, and we arrived at Incheon Airport again at around 5:00 p.m.

It was a miracle they issued my temporary passport on the same day. It was also a miracle that the airline issued a new plane ticket to California for the very next day; after all the chaos, I arrived in California to speak at the three-day conference as scheduled. Thankfully, the conference schedule wasn't changed despite the handbag incident. When I made my schedule a couple months ago, I planned to take a one-day break once I arrived in the U.S. from overseas and before the seminar started. Miraculously as I was able to speak at the conference, and I was so moved and pleased by God's amazing work. Even though I came after ministering in Japan and Korea for two weeks, I wasn't tired at all and I preached with more passion than ever before. I was also told that the conference seemed to manifest God's grace and glory more prominently than before.

Three-Day Inner-Healing Conference at Pastor Ann's House

The three-day conference in Oakland was on fire. Although the conference ended late at night, few women pastors and reverends and deacons took me to a restaurant. Within the group, one of the pastors wanted to invite me again to Northern California for an inner-healing seminar. I gladly accepted and came back in the fall of that year. This time I stayed at Pastor Ann's house in San Jose, and at her house we had the three-day inner healing seminar hosted 25-30 people every evening. On the last day of the seminar, many people didn't leave the house until late at night, and wanted to receive counseling and special prayer from me. I had to leave the house at five in the morning for my flight, however the people did not give me any time to rest. A few people said they wanted more time so they continued to stay with me until 4 a.m.

Unforgettable Incident

Unexpectedly, an unforgettable incident happened. The last person slumped on the floor in front of me. She laid both of her hands comfortably on my lap and said, "Pastor, I am so and so. I really need your help.

Please, do something for me.

I am a regular church member, and also a Bible college student. For a long time, I've been praying to meet a pastor like you. When you were standing on the podium and preaching at the Oakland church, I said, "Lord, I really want to learn from her. God, help me.

After the three evening meetings were over, I wanted to talk to you privately, so I've been anxiously waiting all night for my turn." Then she looked up at me and said, "Pastor, can you please help me?" Suddenly, she dropped her head on my lap saying, "Please Pastor? Can you?"

I willingly reached my hands out to her because I had never seen a person who was so earnest and desperate in my 20 years of national and international ministry. So, I asked her, "Will you obey everything that I tell you and teach you to do?"

She replied, "Yes, I will do everything."

From that day on, she promised to receive my teachings as my disciple, and I also promised to help her as much as I could. After finishing with a blessing prayer, I headed straight to the airport.

Open Door to a New Ministry

Since then, this theology student has been trained by me and she never said "No," when I asked her to come wherever I was speaking and ministering all over the U.S., for about a year. I wanted her to watch and see how I minister in conferences and seminars so she can receive impartation and to learn. After officially graduating from four years of seminary school, she continued to receive my discipleship training and mentorship, and now she is a pastor and missionary in Myanmar.

About thirty people who attended the seminar at Pastor Ann's house, and ten of the intercessors requested that I host an inner healing, restoration, and intercessory prayer seminar three times a year. I gladly accepted.

Actually, I felt the small group would be the perfect idea for an inner healing seminar, because it would be much easier for them to open up about their past hurts and wounds, in order to receive their healing. The Devil tried to obstruct and distract the planned schedule of the Oakland Korean Church conference, but the prayers of our church intercessors and the prayers of the Oakland Korean church brought the spiritual breakthrough that completely defeated the Devil's plans. The Oakland Korean church intercessors have been praying for their local church and the city for a long time, and God's response gave them a total breakthrough. What the enemy meant for evil, God turned for good! When I think about how God poured out His grace upon the Oakland Korean church and their region, it just amazes and astonishes me.

Mentoring Classes That Expanded

What was amazing most of all was that the beginning of Oakland Korean church in California paved the way for me from 2003 to continue to go to Northern California consistently three or four times a year for conferences and seminars centered around intercessory prayer, inner healing, restoration, and leadership training until Covid-19 in 2020.

The original ten people whom I mentored from the beginning all became missionaries and pastors, with one becoming a psalmist (i.e., a worship minister). As news about me spread all over the northern region, every time I visited there were more people gathered than before. I continued to create new small groups and conducted mentoring classes in the same way as the first, second, and third sessions. I also raised up many people as inner healing and intercession ministers. As a result, more than 20 people who officially graduated from seminary school in Northern California are now pastors, teachers, reverends, and missionaries, working together with me to build the kingdom of God. The wonderful thing is, without me realizing, the Holy Spirit has been working greatly to raise up the five-fold ministers who are essential for expanding the Kingdom of God, through me (see Ephesians 4:11-12).

Spiritual Breakthrough #2

July, 2004, The 1st Sunshine International Ministries Intercessory Prayer and Fasting Conference

Since 1989, intercessors from all over the U.S., have gathered in Indiana for a fasting and prayer conference at our church every April. However, God gave me a new vision for the July, 2004, conference under the theme of "Sunshine International Ministries" (SIM Intercessory Prayer and Fasting Conference), which is different from national April fasting and prayer conference. I've invited pastors and their members whom I've met in Korea. I also invited a Japanese pastor and her husband who interpreted my sermons to Japanese for the past two years, when I went to Japan. Also, I had invited the ten intercessors from Northern California who asked me to disciple and raise them spiritually. Twenty people from Korea and Japan and ten people from Northern California traveled long distances with excitement and joy to receive the spiritual breakthrough and impartation.

For the first time they came to Greenfield, Indiana, where my church and home are located. Words could not express the joy of seeing the pastors, missionaries, and lay people who traveled long distances to continue this lasting relationship with me. They were spiritually desperate for a long time.

During the first "SIM Intercessory Prayer and Fasting Conference" that we hosted, we poured out all our might and passion for God to prepare us, and we were ready to welcome Koreans from different states, especially those from other countries. It was like a celebration!

Satan's Timely Attack

The Devil didn't want our visitors to easily join the intercessory prayer and fasting, and receive the spiritual breakthrough. The enemy would never stand back and allow a spiritual breakthrough that would allow these precious people to later become five-fold ministers, who would then be sent into the world to expand the Kingdom of God and open great ministries. Thankfully, the people from Korea and Japan arrived safely two days before the conference.

However, there was an issue with the people who were coming from Northern California. As they were flying to Indiana, the Devil divided them in one way or another and intensely distracted them. Normally, it would take a few hours flying time, but their flight was delayed due to climate change in mid-summer July, which was unusual. The flight wasn't delayed once or twice, but four times, causing them to stay overnight at the airport, and they took more than 30 hours to arrive in Indiana. This incomprehensible situation was absurd, horrifying, and unbelievable, and we know this was spiritual warfare. If these people didn't have the solid determination to receive the anointing of the Holy Spirit for spiritual breakthrough at the Indiana Conference, they would have been disappointed after one or two flight delays and would have returned home. Gratefully, they were prepared and spiritually awake. By having good discernment, they continued to do spiritual warfare and finally arrived in Indiana.

Intercessory Prayer Request with a Desperate Heart

As soon as the people from California arrived in Indiana, they immediately attended meetings, but were both physically and mentally exhausted. I felt extremely sorry for them, and all I could do was to pray. I approached our church intercessors and asked them to, "Please pray for all these people to not be deceived by the Devil, but to be filled by the Holy Spirit. They must return home with complete victory. Pray in your heavenly language for the Devil to be completely defeated." I approached each individual from California and from other countries and said, "Receive the breakthrough. You can't just leave at the end of the conference like this." I hugged them with all my strength, and encouraged each one. Since they longed for the grace of the Lord, I earnestly prayed for them to return home with a fresh breakthrough.

The Result of Intercessory Prayer: Spiritual Breakthrough

On Thursday at 1 pm, the worship minister opened the first day of intercession with words of understanding and Spirit (1Corinthians 14:14-18). As she was leading worship quietly, the fiery work of the Holy Spirit began. I held the mic in front of the congregation and my heart was overwhelmed. "Wow God, I can't believe this is really happening."

For the first time in 32 years since I came to the U.S, it was incredible and truly amazing to see American intercessors from all over the country, Koreans and Japanese from their homeland, and Koreans from California being led by the Holy Spirit to gather for the "SIM Intercessory Prayer and Fasting Conference" in front of me. I told them to find their own, comfortable spot to have a time to examine themselves and pray, and I also went to my own place.

As soon as I sat down, the fire of the Holy Spirit fell upon me. I then went straight to the altar and prostrated myself. I started to travail and pray for breakthrough for those in attendance. One by one, those who watched me travail in prayer began to fall by the power of the Holy Spirit. Several people came to the altar, prostrated themselves, and cried out loud, "Jesus! Father!" Here and there, they raised their voices, crying out and bursting into tears. At one point, the attendees were all weeping and wailing in travail. As the same thing happened repeatedly during every sermon and intercession, everyone said they received more grace than they hoped for, and they promised to return every year.

Our adversary was once again defeated by the prayers of the intercessors. Those who came experienced the miracle of encountering the Lord in His presence and received the breakthrough.

International Prayer and Fasting Conference

By faith I obeyed the Lord during the "International Intercessory Prayer and Fasting Conference" in July 2004, and the fruits of that obedience were greater than I expected. From that conference onward, the April conference that was attended mainly by Americans for 15 years has now become an "International Prayer and Fasting Conference." Every year, the number of attendees has increased, and the news about my ministry has spread throughout Korean communities in many states.

Spiritual Battle Brings Spiritual Breakthrough

Spiritual battle and spiritual breakthrough are inseparable. Those who want spiritual breakthrough *must* go through spiritual battle. In order to have victory, there is a definite price to pay. What intercessors must remember is that whenever we go through a new door of ministry, we must prepare for a new spiritual battle. Our adversary is always ready to attack us with all kinds of methods and tactics to stop us from starting a new work of God. The Devil doesn't want us to take back the territory, family, and ministry that he's stolen, and he will resist us from setting foot in any new territory. What we must also remember is that when we are experiencing an intense spiritual battle, we can then expect an even greater spiritual breakthrough. The greater the war, the greater the victory!

Spiritual Breakthrough #3

The Power of Intercessory Prayer Testimony: Kay, Mrs. Beauty Queen

Meeting the Beautiful Korean Lady for the First Time

The news of my discipleship training and mentoring in Northern California soon spread to Los Angeles, Southern California. One day, I received a request to be a guest speaker for a Holy Spirit Revival meeting at a location close to L.A. This Revival meeting was hosted by Reverend Lee, and had a little over 50 people in attendance. At this meeting, I preached sermons and gave prophetic words to many. At the meeting, God allowed me to meet someone with whom I would have a lifelong relationship.

When I first met her, Kay was so beautiful and tall that I wondered if she had ever entered a Miss Korea contest in Korea. Although she was among many, she had such a unique beauty that caught my attention. Later, I found out that when she was younger, she won the first place in Mrs. Korea contest held in Los Angeles, California. She told me that she was divorced and a single parent raising a young son by herself. Even though it was my first time seeing her, the Holy Spirit gave me the impression that, "She's a woman but definitely a warrior."

When I first laid my hands on Kay to pray, I asked, "Are you ministering a church?"

"Yes," she replied.

Then I continued, "I don't know what you are currently doing; however, God gave me a word that you are the one who will answer His calling to go out to the mission field and give testimony and sermons to many nations, and bring great glory to God."

Then Kay replied, "I don't want to be a reverend or a pastor, but I've been dreaming of going on a short-term mission ministry as a regular lay minister."

As she handed me her phone number, she requested that I contact her whenever I visit L.A. again, and that she would host a dinner. However, as if I had known this person all my life, my heart became comfortable, and I felt as if I would see her more often in the future. I was looking forward to visiting her again in Los Angeles.

The Beginning of My Los Angeles Ministry

After a couple months, I met Kay again in L.A., and she requested that I frequently come to minister, since there were so many people around her who needed inner-healing and restoration. I requested small group of people for the purpose of more personal and intimate setting for inner healing and deliverance. She gathered more than ten of her closest friends, which ignited a spark and I continued to go to L.A., to hold inner-healing and intercessory prayer seminars. In these meetings, I repeated the same ministry method and teaching that I had used in Northern California. As a result, I saw the same manifestations in that place like the ones I've seen in other places.

Kay continued to invite me to hold inner healing and intercessory seminars and prayer meetings three times a year for seven years. She also advertised the ministry in newspapers for people who were emotionally hurt and in of need restoration to receive inner-healing and breakthroughs. There were newcomers every time and the number of people who came to receive teaching, prayer and at times personal counseling grew each meeting. God's work started to rise in Los Angeles and in Southern California as well. The meeting grew every time I went. Kay was very faithful to her local church and well loved by the pastor of her local church, but she also had a good relationship with many other pastors and introduced me to them. This opened an opportunity to hold conferences and seminars at their churches.

A Shocking Truth

Kay was a warrior, I always told her she is called to be a general for Christ because she was a hard worker in everything she did. Wherever she went, she was popular among many because of her cool and outgoing personality. Before she met me, she had been active in the women's ministry in her church for a long time. She didn't hesitate to help others whenever she had money in her pocket, always buying them things and relentlessly giving. Kay was a faithful prayer warrior who attended most morning prayer meetings, read the Word daily, and went to church regularly. But there was one big problem: She was addicted to alcohol.

Christian Alcoholic

Kay had a serious drinking problem. She loved to drink so much that once she started, she would keep going until blacking out. Since she worked as a realtor in L.A, the real estate industry was aware of the long-time rumor that this beautiful woman was a heavy drinker. Although I visited L.A. several times, I would never have imagined that she would be a heavy drinker.

When people heard the news that I was partnering with Kay to do inner-healing and intercessory prayer ministry, I received a couple calls of criticism.

"Pastor Sun, did you know that Kay is a heavy drinker? Because of her, Christians are getting a bad reputation. Every night, she goes out with men to the bar and while being fully drunk, she boasts about how she's a Christian who attends the morning prayer. Does this make sense?"

"Pastor Sun, I think you are so naive. You're even getting a bad reputation because of her, and I suggest you avoid Kay as soon as possible before it greatly affects your ministry. Even if I want to attend your healing ministry, I can't go because I don't want to see her."

Hearing all this, I came before God and asked, "What should I do?"

Immediately He replied, *"Think about what kind of ministry you've been doing so far: Inner-healing, restoration, and intercessory prayer. Then, think about what you can do for Kay."*

Suddenly, I remembered so clearly the first day when I gave her a prophetic prayer. "God is showing me that you received a calling to go to the missionary fields and give testimonies to many nations, and bring great glory to God."

Intercessory Prayer Proclaiming God's Calling for Kay

As soon as I realized the reason I met Kay, I started to intercede. Because I met her through the guidance of the Holy Spirit, I had confident faith that the Holy Spirit will also help me to intercede for her. I declared with faith that Jesus would set Kay free from alcohol addiction.

Whenever I visited Los Angeles, there were many people who liked and loved Kay. There were also many people who criticized her behind her back about her alcohol problem. After praying for all people who attended one of my meetings and seminars, I would always lay my hands on Kay and pray for her in a private room. At times, I would give a travailing prayer, proclaiming that this would be the last prayer that would set her free from alcoholism. Every time I returned home after the meetings and praying for her, she would call me saying she hasn't drunk for one to two weeks, which was good news. However, I pressed on to intercede until she was completely delivered from alcoholism.

What I was grateful for was that people who loved Kay wanted to come together with one heart to intercede with me. Kay, who was enslaved by alcoholism for a long time, still continued to drink for a few more years even after working with me. Ironically, she said that no matter how drunk she got, and even if she drank until dawn, she would never fail to get up when it was time to go to morning prayer. And she always prayed the same, "Jesus, you know how much I love you right? Don't let me quit drinking by getting injured or getting sick, but help me to naturally quit."

Love of Alcohol, Love of Jesus

Whenever we gathered for fellowship, Kay always loudly boasted, "Nobody knows how much I love God. Only Jesus knows how I cry out to God during the morning prayer. But no matter how much I want to quit, I can't control it. What do you want me to do?" It was the same scenario every time.

At one prayer gathering, God gave me a word for Kay: "If you really love Jesus, you cannot continue to drink like this. The Lord showed me that you love alcohol more than Jesus. How can you quit since you love alcohol more than Jesus? No matter how much we pray for you, you can't escape from alcoholism unless you hate it and let go of it. Loving alcohol more than Jesus means that you are loving the Devil as much."

Hearing this, Kay couldn't give any excuse and nodded her head saying, "Yes, Pastor. I understand well."

Los Angeles Korean Church

In September 2008, I held a four-day inner-healing and intercessory prayer conference at a Korean church in Los Angeles that was again introduced by Kay. It was exactly the fourth year of meeting her. By the presence of the Holy Spirit, the message of my sermon and testimony touched many people who repented, and received inner-healing and deliverance. Korean churches held early intercessory prayer every morning. The great fire that fell on early morning prayer meeting and the ministry led many to be baptized in the Holy Spirit and to speak in a heavenly language. The morning prayer was also part of the conference. People who attended all three nights and morning prayers would burst into tears and weep as I came down from the pulpit to minister to them. About 150 people were in the sanctuary, and the place turned into a sea of tears, echoing with cries from the people. Thankfully, Kay was in every meeting, and I prayed and travailed for her every chance I had. She was very touched and blessed as well with many others.

True Freedom from Alcohol Addiction

I continued to pray for many until the following day, Sunday, and successfully ended the conference, then returned home. A couple weeks later, Kay called me, and her voice was different than before. "Pastor! It's real this time. After you returned home, I haven't had a drop of alcohol on my lips since then."

It had been about eleven years since she's been fighting the spiritual battle with the Devil of alcohol addiction, and she finally received a breakthrough and won a complete victory. She has been free from alcohol addiction for more than 14 years.

If we don't judge our loved ones and continue to embrace them through intercessory prayer, then one day our prayers will bear beautiful fruit.

The Famous Drinker in Los Angeles Becomes a Beautiful Pastor and Missionary

When Kay first saw me, she said that she would never become a reverend or a pastor, but as I went through discipleship with her, she changed her heart. She wasn't satisfied with being a regular church member, so she accepted God's calling on her life to be His servant. Her desperate prayers were answered through His mercy and grace. She didn't get hurt, sick, or had an accident to quit but the Holy Spirit guided her to stop drinking spontaneously.

After being alcohol-free, God led her to pray all night and trained her for five years to put down her ego and to be a powerful intercessor who embraces the local church, Southern California, and the nations. Subsequently, she officially graduated from seminary and became a reverend after ten years of knowing me, and three years later she traveled to nine different countries as a short-term missionary to testify and minister. As God raised Kay to be a full-time minister, He also tremendously blessed her only son. He graduated from a well-known medical school in California as a scholarship student, and now works in a large hospital as a well-recognized doctor in California. When I see how her very first prophetic prayer is actively being fulfilled in her life, I see how great God is once again.

God's Everlasting Love

I'm so grateful to God for allowing me to witness the growth of the people who have been part of my discipleship training in Southern California. They started as layman, but eventually graduated seminary and now are actively leading their own ministry as a five-fold minister. Kay continues in her dual callings of pastor and a missionary, and heads out towards the world with God's vision in her heart. I believe this is the result of the intercessory prayer on behalf of our beloved Missionary, Pastor Kay. God's everlasting love and faithfulness leads me to my knees.

CHAPTER 11

QUALITIES OF AN INTERCESSOR

The Qualities of an Intercessor

1. Intercessory Prayer from the Heart

Just as we give our hearts to our loved ones, we must open our hearts to the ones for whom we are interceding. God desires true intercessors who pray with an attitude that cares for others above themselves. God gave us His only begotten Son, and Jesus gave His life to send the Holy Spirit to us. The Holy Spirit never boasts on Himself but manifests glory to God and Jesus Christ.

The more we yield to the Holy Spirit within us, we will naturally be emptied of ourselves and consider others first.

God always desires to bless us and that is the Father God's heart. Do not be content by giving Him just material offerings, or showing loyalty and service. God wants us to be the ones who give our whole hearts.

2. Faithful Character and a Clean Heart

A faithful character and a clean heart allow us to love sincerely. Sincere love enables us to intercede with power that moves the hand of God. A righteous and a pure prayer is a prayer that acknowledges God alone. It is the prayer of one who always wants to please God in everything and to glorify Him. And God answers these prayers of the righteous and the pure (Proverbs 15:29). There is no power in the prayer of the one who has a hidden sin (James 5:16). Unless we have an upright heart before God, our prayers won't be heard (Psalm 51). If we only *think* about having a changed heart before God or only *desire* for God's character, that is not enough. We must be willing to make the sacrifices God calls us to make. We must crucify our flesh (Galatians 5:24), and actively find the distractions that stop our prayers from being answered.

3. A Person Who Endures Sacrifice and Devotion

Just as love requires devotion and sacrifice, intercession also requires devotion and sacrifice. True intercessors willingly surrender their time, heart, and body to pray for their loved ones, their church, which is the local body of Christ, their neighbors, and their nation. Intercessors are truly beautiful people, because they are the ones who make sacrifices and dedicate themselves to the benefit of others. That is why there's something truly different about intercessors.

These are the people who can give their time and can completely lay down themselves for others. At times, they pray hard, even going through travailing prayer. Ultimately, these people are not self-centered. They always have others in mind; if others are happy, they are happy too. Even if people don't acknowledge their work, they are thankful when they see God answering their prayers and blessing others, and this becomes their testimony. This is the true meaning and reward of intercession: God is rejoicing over this intercessor's sacrificial heart and He happily receives their prayers. Unfortunately, many Christians are not interceding because they have yet to taste this blessing.

> *(Ephesians 6:18) "Praying always with all prayer and supplication in the Spirit, being watchful to this end with all perseverance and supplication for all the saints."*

4. A Person Beyond Themselves

True love does not seek its own (1 Corinthians 13:5). A true intercessor does not seek their own benefits. When asked, "How long have you been a Christian?" They might answer, "For several years."

Throughout Christendom, there are many who are still stuck on the level of seeking only, "me, me, me." Oftentimes, we see that those who are praying only for themselves are oppressed; their prayers are focused on themselves so there is no growth. Because a self-centered person primarily thinks only about their needs and wants instead of caring about the conditions of the people around them, whether they are dying or sick, they become ignorant of Satan's devices (2 Corinthians 2:11).

(Philippians 2:3-4) "Let nothing be done through selfish ambition or conceit, but in lowliness of mind let each esteem others better than himself. Let each of you look out not only for his own interests, but also for the interests of others."

A Lesson Learned

In my case, I had this experience. When my ex-daughter-in-law was in the delivery room to give birth, I continued to pray in my spiritual language in front of her. All of a sudden, she whispered in my son's ear, and he told me to stop praying because it made her feel uncomfortable. I was somewhat upset with her for telling me to stop praying because I was trying to support her. In my mind I said, "Lord, I was only praying for her to give birth smoothly; how can she do this to me?"

And God answered right away: *"Why do you always have to do it your way?"*

God is the One who teaches us who to pray for, what to pray, and how to pray. But oftentimes we pray in our own convenient ways. We are rebelling against God when we pray in our own stubbornness, without the guidance of the Holy Spirit, and without considering the other person's heart. The quality of a true intercessor is to lay down everything, even our own methods of prayer.

5. One Who Only Depends on God

We cannot truly love our neighbors without knowing God's love. Likewise, we cannot truly intercede if we do not rely on God's love. We are all humans with limitations. We cannot have an intimate relationship with God nor experience the spiritual realm with our own might. The Holy Spirit is forever with us. The Holy Spirit knows our weaknesses and He enables us to enter God's presence to meet with Him. Once we experience the presence of God, our lives will be changed. When this happens, we can love the ones whom we couldn't love, and our enemies will begin to look lovable. Even if we are surrounded by worries and oppressed in our circumstances, ultimately we will not be crushed, but receive the faith to focus on God.

> (Proverbs 3:5-6) "Trust in the Lord with all your heart, and lean not on your own understanding; In all your ways acknowledge Him, and He shall direct your paths."

6. One Who Acknowledge Each Other's Needs

There are certain attitudes we need when we are interceding. For example, we must acknowledge the fact that we need each other. It's a heart that says, "I need your prayer and you need my prayer. So, I will pray for you, can you pray for me?"

After we receive salvation, we must remember the truth that we need to help one another in order to expand the kingdom of God. Some say, "I don't need other people, I just need God." Most often, these people have been hurt by other Christians, and are unwilling to allow God to heal their wounds.

At times, God works in our lives by using people we may not like. When God speaks that I need them and they need me, despite what I think, I must open my heart, receive it fully and humbly obey. It is a blessing to be someone who can help those in need, and to receive help from another. A revelation from the Word that is given to us from another is timely, uplifting and can be healing. But if we ignore the person and the word given, we will become lonely and feel isolated.

> *(Ephesians 4:16) "From whom the whole body, joined and knit together by what every joint supplies, according to the effective working by which every part does its share, causes growth of the body for the edifying of itself in love."*

7. One Who Has a Teachable Attitude

One of the most important qualities of an intercessor to have is a teachable attitude. We need to have a heart to obey and be willing to learn from the people who are living by the guidance of the Lord. All of us must receive teaching and guidance. The ones who think they know all things, even though they know little, will resist learning and are full of pride and gripped by their egos. The fact is, there is always someone who is more spiritual than us. It is dangerous to think of oneself as, "I can do all things by myself," or, "I know everything." This thinking is a scary illness. What God wants from us is a humble, teachable heart. However, we can't be teachable when we have a heart posture of, "I'm better than you," or, "I'm smarter than you." If we truly desire to be teachable, we should learn even from little children. It is unwise to refuse to be taught. We can accumulate knowledge by reading books. But no matter how much we know, it is in vain if we cannot teach and learn from each other through human relationships. We need to widely open our hearts and minds to always learn.

> *(Proverbs 16:18) "Pride goes before destruction, and a haughty spirit before a fall."*
>
> *(Proverbs 1:2-5) "To know wisdom and instruction, to perceive the words of understanding, to receive the instruction of wisdom,*

justice, judgment, and equity; to give prudence to the simple, to the young man knowledge and discretion—A wise man will hear and increase learning, and a man of understanding will attain wise counsel."

8. A Humble Attitude

Many gifts follow those who intercede. For instance, there are the gifts of prophecy, dreams, visions, and hearing and seeing revelation. These gifts are given to be used for others during intercessory prayer; however, we often see people using these gifts to boast about themselves. They speak as if they are the only ones who are gifted and spiritual. Sadly, I also made these kinds of mistakes many times in the past. In the beginning of my ministry, when I would do inner healing prayer, I would often offend the individual, and I would have to clean up after my mistakes.

Many times, I've prayed and God has given me a prophetic dream to show me something, and spoke to me through that dream. I was excited, so I found the individual and shared what God had shown me. For example, I was praying for a young woman when God showed me something about her life. I then went to her and said, "You must pray. God showed me this: As I was praying for you, I saw you at the bar dancing with a man and that man, without any care." However, the woman replied with an anger, "What kind of crazy God would show you about my personal life?"

Of course, if she was ready to receive my words, she would be honest and say, "Oh really? God really gave you that dream?" Then she would surrender and humble herself.

But my harshness and prideful attitudes drove her away from church and God.

Another time I told a young person, "God gave me a dream. Your house is full of trash. God told me that this is your spiritual condition. Quickly repent and clean up your spiritual mess, otherwise, you will be in trouble."

Once again, my tone and attitude were harsh, and my immature action were not received.

No matter how seriously I spoke to these people, they were unable to receive my words. Instead, they were angry and left the church. Since I frequently had trouble in the relationships with the church members, I cried out to the Lord. In His great grace towards me, the Lord said, *"The dream and revelation I showed you was for you to intercede for that person. It wasn't for you to boast about how spiritual you are. I can't encourage you with your prideful heart."* Later, I realized that people rejected and didn't accept my words because I didn't relay my message with a humble motive, but was trying to show how spiritual I was.

God taught me a valuable lesson through that experience His word found in James 4:10 has stayed with me to this day: *"Humble yourselves before the Lord, and he will lift you up."*

Whenever I visit a church for a conference, I always request to see their intercessor leader. In most churches, the pastors would say, "I am the intercessory leader."

I would then ask, "Why don't you raise an intercessory leader?"

Often the pastor would tell me that the head intercessors were making lots of trouble, so the pastor himself decided to lead the people. The intercessors' job was to humble themselves, pray, and serve the church. Instead, they became prideful with the gifts that God gave them, and wounded the church members and/or leadership with their prophecy.

Every intercessor must take what God has shown them as a precious to His heart. God has chosen to entrust us with something very dear to Him, and we need to humble ourselves even more and pray. Yes, we make mistakes because we are human; however, being prideful over what God has shown us or delivering a harsh word because we feel we are "spiritual" does not represent the heart of God. Even if the testimonies of our answered prayers are glowing, we must always remember to *only* glorify God. No matter how fantastic the vision or revelation that God may show us, if we are not humble, we will be hurtful. That is why intercessors must especially be alert of a prideful heart and ceaselessly go through the practice of putting down their egos. The attitude of the intercessors is to find joy only in the Lord. Then the intercessors will become treasures in their church.

> *(1Peter 5:6) "Therefore humble yourselves under the mighty hand of God, that He may exalt you in due time."*
>
> *(James 4:6) "But He gives more grace. Therefore He says: 'God resists the proud, but gives grace to the humble.'"*

9. Intercessors Are Rooted in the Word

When we are faced with tests and trials, the word sown within us will bear fruit that glorifies God. However, if the Word is not sown within us, we will be confused about the God we are serving and our identity in Him when we are attacked by the Devil.

> *(Matthew 13:18-23) "Therefore hear the parable of the sower: When anyone hears the word of the kingdom, and does not understand it, then the wicked one comes and snatches away what was sown in his heart. This is he who received seed by the wayside. But he who received the seed on stony places, this is he who hears the word and immediately receives it with joy; yet he has no root in himself, but endures only for a while. For when tribulation or persecution arises because of the word, immediately he stumbles. Now he who received seed among the thorns is he who hears the word, and the cares of this world and the deceitfulness of riches choke the word, and he becomes unfruitful. But he who received seed on the good ground is he who hears the word and understands it, who indeed bears fruit and produces: some a hundredfold, some sixty, some thirty."*
>
> *(1Peter 2:2) "As newborn babes, desire the pure milk of the word, that you may grow thereby."*

10. One Who Received Inner-Healing

Just like an emotionally or spiritually wounded person can't love their neighbors freely, an intercessor who has not received inner healing cannot pray fully for their neighbors. If we carry resentment or bitterness in our hearts, we will only be focused on our own problems and won't have compassion for others. When bitterness is sown and rooted within us, we won't be able to pray as God desires, we will lack any progress in our prayer time, and we will be unable to bear fruit that will last (Hebrews 12:15; John 15:16). Once our hearts are emptied of "self" and receive God's heart, we can begin to pray sincerely for others. Without receiving God's heart, we can't pray with a burning heart. As well, only after we forgive the person who is causing us grief can we pray for that individual (Colossians 3:13). To intercede effectively, we must first acknowledge the wounds within us and ask the Holy Spirit to pull out any root of unforgiveness and bitterness. Once we have received God's inner-healing and freedom, we can truly lift up the prayer of intercession that God desires.

> *(Matthew 6:14-15) "For if you forgive men their trespasses, your heavenly Father will also forgive you. But if you do not forgive men their trespasses, neither will your Father forgive your trespasses."*

(Recommended for readers who need inner healing) Authored by Sun Fannin

1. *The Bad Luck Baby*, my testimony
2. *If My* People: Inner-Healing Through Fasting and Prayer
3. *This Too Will Pass*, the sequel to *The Bad Luck Baby*
4. *The Flow of God's Grace in the Wilderness*
5. *Inner-Healing and Restoration*, Restoration Series

CHAPTER 12

THE POWER OF INTERCESSORY PRAYER TESTIMONY: THE BREAKTHROUGH OF THE JAPANESE PEOPLE

The Door Opens for Intercessory Prayer Ministry in Japan

While I was busy with the ministry all over the United States and visiting Korea, God widened the scope and allowed me to enter through a new door of ministry. A former president and elder (now a pastor) of the publishing company "Chariots of Fire" handed my Korean book *The Bad Luck Baby* to Pastor Kim who was serving as a long-time missionary in Japan. After reading my book, he invited me as a guest speaker to a prophetic intercessory prayer conference in Tokyo, Japan.

In 2002, I visited Japan for the first time and preached in English with a Japanese interpreter beside me. As soon as another speaker finished her speech, I stood on the podium with a fluttering heart and excitement; this was my first time speaking in Tokyo, Japan. I continued the flow of the conference, and I was able to finish my sermon. Thankfully, the reaction of the Japanese people was more fervent than I thought. According to Pastor Kim, it was very unusual in Japanese culture to have a Christian conference with over a several hundred people. He was very excited and invited me back to Japan to another conference in Osaka within six months. That meeting again gathered hundreds of people, and Pastor Kim was so pleased, he continued to invite me to Japan.

The Lament of the Holy Spirit Towards Japan

Again, God began to work way beyond my imagination. Whenever I visited Japan, I couldn't hold back my feelings towards the souls in Japan. Every time we held a conference or a seminar, the Holy Spirit gave me a heart for the Japanese people, and led me to lament and into travailing prayer for them. I poured out my heart with tears as I prayed for the Japanese people during every conference. On the podium, I preached with all my heart and appealed to the audience with tears streaming down my face. I exhort them to have intercessory prayer for souls to be saved, and to evangelize for Japan's revival. I also encouraged them to intercede for their nation. I strongly challenged them that unless the Japanese Christians fasted and interceded for their nation and people, then who else would do it? It seemed like they had never heard a preacher like me. At first, seeing a foreigner weeping and travailing for the revival of their nation. They seemed not to know what to do and looked like they were pondering my words. However, soon after, they began to join me and we wept and prayed together for their nation and people.

The Expansion of Ministry in Japan

I didn't have any idea how great God's plan was when I stepped into Japan under the guidance of the Holy Spirit. For a long time, Pastor Kim, a missionary in Japan, invited many speakers from overseas to the conference he hosted for the revival of the churches in Japan. And he asked that I visit Japan more often, even with my busy schedule, because he said it was uncommon to see a speaker like me. In addition, he took me all over the region to churches filled with his disciples, whom he spiritually raised for many years, to do seminars on intercessory prayer, inner-healing, and restoration.

Interceding For Japan's Revival

Since 2002, I have visited Japan regularly four to five times every year and traveled to each region, leading intercessory prayer seminars. However, since 2004, I have joined hands with Pastor A, the founder of Revival Ministries, who regularly hosted "Intercessory Prayer Leadership Seminars" for three days in spring, summer, and fall. As well, Revival Ministries hosted a two-day conference where hundreds of people gathered, and I was invited as a speaker many times.

We gathered in the large auditorium in Tokyo, and I ministered to many who came from all over Japan, after seeing an advertisement in a Christian magazine. In two-day conference I preached several times. I also prayed prophetic prayers and deliverance prayers for many people who were possessed by a spirit due to mental and physical illness. And to those who need spiritual awakening

In the spring of 2013, during the intercessory prayer leadership seminar, I was inspired by the Holy Spirit to challenge the Japanese people. I told them of my three-day fasting and prayer conference hosted by Sunshine Ministries every year in America. I encouraged them to pray about coming to receive a spiritual breakthrough. Most important, I said this because I believed Japanese Christians needed to experience a spiritual breakthrough by the flow of the Holy Spirit and to be transformed by His grace. Although the host of the seminar told me to freely preach and do ministry, but I felt limited because I still had to follow their time schedule and couldn't let the Holy Spirit fully work through me. I wanted them to experience the freedom and the powerful anointing of the Holy Spirit, especially through the fasting and prayer conference in America.

Less Than One Percent

While weeping and embracing the Japanese people, I poured out my heart as I led numerous intercessory prayer and prophetic ministry meetings. No matter how I pondered about them, the prayers and the tears I wept were beyond my comprehension; They were an expression of Jesus' heart and love for the Japanese people.

However, every time I visited Japan, the feeling of discontent grew stronger. There were regular members who always attended every intercessory prayer leadership seminar, but somehow, I felt those in attendance were not growing spiritually. As well, despite seeing some members several times per year and doing my best to minister to them, unfortunately, except for a few people, I didn't see much transformation in them. Most of all, my heart ached and was sad because it seemed like they didn't know the true peace, joy, and freedom in Christ Jesus. Catholics and Christians represent less than one percent of the 130 million Japanese population, and it is rare to see Christians who rely on the Holy Spirit to pray.

At one of my conferences, a Japanese missionary told me there are eight million idols in Japan. The Japan I saw—and see today—is spiritually very dark and is heavily oppressed. Many are oppressed mentally, physically, and even emotionally, and as the days went by, the love of God for the souls in Japan increased within me. Whenever I interceded, whether at home or in Japan, I couldn't pray without uncontrollably weeping for the nation. Ultimately, because of my yearning heart for these people, I recommended them to visit America for the fasting and prayer conference.

Strong Dedication and Commitment of the Japanese People

I shared the testimony to the Japanese people of how the intercessors from all over the states and the pastors who flew all the way from Korea yearly for the fasting and prayer conference, experienced many breakthroughs as they faced spiritual warfare and received the anointing of the Holy Spirit. I was the person who strongly challenged them to come to America to join the spiritual work, and I was shocked to see the outcome of the challenge. In April 2014, exactly the 10th year of starting Revival Ministries with Pastor A, I received a call that 36 people had booked a flight to join the fasting and prayer conference saying that they wanted to experience the movement of the Holy Spirit and spiritual breakthroughs.

A Change in Ministry Direction

In 2014, an unexpected incident greatly challenged me. Thirty-six Japanese people were attending my Sunshine Ministries Conference in Indiana. My late husband, Pastor Larry, suggested preparing meals for the guests who were coming, and to change the fasting and prayer conference to an intercessory prayer conference. Because they were coming from overseas, he felt we should feed our guests, unless they wanted to fast through mealtimes. I then requested my church intercessors and a few pastors whom I trust to intercede for the will of God for this new direction for my yearly conference.

After praying for several days, the answers my intercessors received were the same as Pastor Larry's. It was undoubtedly God's guidance. I also had the same heart. I recommended to those who wanted to fast to individually to obey the leading of the Holy Spirit. But I also felt inspired to feed physically and spiritually those whose goal wasn't to fast, but to participate in intercessory prayer. As soon as we received the confirmation and the inspiration, we began to put this change in direction into action. This was first time in 25 years that my fasting and prayer conference changed to an intercessory prayer conference. I emailed pastor A about the changes we had made; amazingly, she was glad to hear that we have changed. She was concerned about some people who never experienced fast would be too hard on them while their visit to America.

Voluntary Dedication and Service

As soon as our church heard that 36 Japanese people were coming to America for the first time just to attend our conference, the excitement grew. Knowing that people from the United States, Korea, and Japan were attending the first ever International Intercessory Prayer Conference, the church members were full of joy. Many approached me and asked, "What can I do to help you? I can take some days off from work." God's work was so amazing and exciting that it was beyond my imagination. As this was a new ministry, our church's Intercessory Prayer Team met frequently and prayed diligently, and we rushed to finish meal preparation, something that our church had never done before.

The Japanese People Arrive

We created a one-week schedule for the Japanese people, from Tuesday night to the following Tuesday morning, including the three-day intercessory prayer conference. Unlike our Korean guests, the Japanese attendees didn't want to share their room with more than two people, and many wanted to have their own room. This made the cost of the hotel rooms for a week quite expensive for each person; however, they didn't worry about the cost. The only thing they desired was to experience the Holy Spirit and spiritual breakthrough.

An Unexpected Emergency

Finally, the 36 Japanese people arrived in America two days before the conference. However, the Japanese people arrived in Chicago, an unforeseen situation occurred. The beautiful April weather suddenly changed to severe winds and storms, and their flight to Indiana was delayed. Waiting six hours might be nothing to a younger person, but to older people it was not an easy task. Only three of the 36 people had visited America before, and many newcomers came from the Japanese countryside, where they had to take buses and trains to travel long distances to arrive at Narita Airport. Many of them did not sleep for thirty hours or more, and were exhausted from waiting in the Chicago airport.

Confronting the Devil

The news I heard from the Chicago airport was unbelievable. Gradually, my chest tightened with uneasiness and I was fearful. "Oh Lord! Please help us. They came to receive spiritual breakthroughs but are being attacked by the Devil and are being tempted, even before the conference starts. And they are saying that some of them are sick! How can they receive breakthroughs if they are lying in bed during the week of the conference? Please, touch them, Lord."

Then, I began to confront the Devil with a loud voice. "I command all the powers of darkness and principalities distracting the Japanese people's spiritual breakthroughs to go in Jesus' name! All you devils, I rebuke your demonic schemes against them and command you to be gone, in Jesus' name!" I yelled at the top of my lungs and continued to earnestly pray in tongues without ceasing.

Once they left Chicago, these bewildered people had a one-hour flight and a one-hour drive before arriving in Greenfield and checking into the hotel. The unexpected cold weather also caused many of them numerous body aches and some to catch a cold. I was at home eagerly awaiting their arrival, but when I answered the phone, I was told, "Pastor, so-and-so is sick and so-and-so is full of complaining."

Disunity of the Thirty-Six

The problem was these people were all from different churches and didn't know each other well. Some came to America because they wanted to experience the Holy Spirit and were desperate to receive a spiritual breakthrough; but there were some older members who just followed their children to America so that they could tour. In this unexpected situation, the unity and the order turned into chaos from Chicago airport all the way to the Greenfield hotel, with the people resentful and complaining towards one another. Since they were already physically exhausted, it seemed they were unable to unite and pray to engage in spiritual warfare.

I remembered past conferences, and I recalled experiencing so much spiritual warfare; I knew that the Japanese people were getting attacked by the Devil as soon as they arrived in America. It was so clear that he was trying to prevent and distract these precious people from experiencing the Holy Spirit and spiritual breakthrough. Immediately, I called our church Intercessory Prayer Team to pray fervently and fight in this spiritual battle.

To attend the conference on Thursday, we scheduled the Japanese attendees to fully rest on Wednesday because of the thirteen-hour time difference from Japan. From Thursday to Saturday, they would attend the three-day conference. After joining our Sunday morning service, they were scheduled to go shopping and have a day of sightseeing until Monday, then fly back to Japan on Tuesday morning. However, the weather in Indiana was unusually windy and cold, and more than half of the people were stuck in their rooms, due to feeling sick.

The Side Effect of The Cold Medicine

Unfortunately, those who weren't feeling well could not go to the hospital, so I rushed to the pharmacy and bought cold, cough, body ache medicines for them but a bigger problem arose. They said American medicine was stronger than Japanese medicine, so they became drowsy and suffered side effects. As the time passed, the problem grew and their disappointment and frustration became visible. With desperation in my heart, I ran into the church and prostrated myself before the altar. For a long time, I spoke in tongues and engaged in spiritual battle.

Proclaiming in Faith Against the Devil

With tears covering my face, I cried out loud. I fervently prayed that this would not be a wasted trip for Japanese people, and that God's grace would be poured out on them so they would receive a tremendous experience of the Holy Spirit and the spiritual breakthrough.

While I was praying, I became extremely angry against the Devil who was relentlessly oppressing God's people and preventing them from entering His presence. I thought if these people returned home without a victory, they would become the Devil's target forever, and they wouldn't be able to withstand his accusations and the ridicule. Then I stood up and said, "Devil, I command in the name of Jesus, to loosen the Japanese Christians! They will not return home without their spiritual breakthrough! No, it will never happen!" I continued to declare in faith. After a good spiritual fight, I felt refreshed.

The next day was the first day of the Intercessory Prayer Conference. It began with an intercessory prayer session at 1 pm and thankfully, except for one person, those who were sick felt well enough to attend the meeting.

Heaven's Celebration

During intercession, I requested the intercessors, pastors, and ministers attending from all over the states and Korea to focus on praying for the Japanese church to experience the Holy Spirit and the spiritual breakthrough. Intercessors began to lay their hands on the Japanese attendees and passionately prayed for them. On the second day at 9 am during the intercessory prayer time, the intercessors again laid their hands on the Japanese people and sincerely prayed for them. Although they spoke different languages and couldn't understand each other, they were united in one spirit, and they wept and embraced each other. Finally, the Holy Spirit began to work. During the afternoon service of the second day, while everyone was praising God in fiery worship, the expressions of the Japanese people began to change from fear and depression to joy and amazement, as an amazing breakthrough began.

The Moment of Spiritual Breakthrough

The atmosphere of the conference was like heaven's celebration. The people lifted their voices in worship and some people danced in worship. Others encountered the true freedom in Christ and jumped and danced like children. On one side, several people held hands and went in circles like the Jewish people danced. As the Japanese people watched with admiration, they soon took a step forward and joined the dance. By the third day, the Japanese people danced and met God afresh in heaven's celebration. Finally, they experienced the Holy Spirit and the breakthrough they desired. It was a rare and precious sight that was uncommon in the Japanese churches.

Stronger From Continuous Spiritual Warfare

The enemy tried to disappoint the Japanese people until the very end. Because of the harsh climate, again, their return flight to Japan was delayed for another day, and all the 36 people had to stay at a hotel near the airport. For many years, I've been flying and experienced some flight delays, but one-day delays are rare. The amazing fact was, unlike the first day they arrived in America, they didn't lose the grace they received from the conference; instead, they spent an extra beautiful day sharing the grace they received with one another.

In the years that followed, the Japanese people returned to the conference yearly, and always faced spiritual warfare at some level. While this was not easy for them, they were determined to receive spiritual breakthroughs and to experience the Holy Spirit in fresh and new ways.

Satan's Continuous Attacks

In 2015, Pastor A, who was the leader of Revival Ministries in Japan, came to the conference for the second time with twenty Japanese people. But this time, each person who attended longed for the work of the Holy Spirit. These people had tasted the Holy Spirit and wanted to receive their spiritual breakthrough again, so they came with greater expectations to America than the previous year. Together, with a few pastors and church members, thankfully, they safely arrived at the hotel with excitement and joy. Their hearts were opened from the first day of the conference, so they received grace from the start. The Holy Spirit touched their hearts and worked miraculously because their hearts were fully opened. I was really satisfied and happy since the first day of the conference was powerful and overflowing with God's grace, and I joyfully returned home with greater anticipation for tomorrow. Yet again, Satan began to attack the Japanese people terribly.

The Midnight Call

It was past midnight and while I was getting ready for bed my phone rang. I wondered who would call this late at night, so I quickly picked up the phone. Surprisingly it was one of the Japanese people. "Pastor, it's an emergency! There's a flood in the hotel. The fire truck just arrived, and they are trying to take out the water from the hallway of the hotel to outside."

I rushed out of my house and jumped into my car and arrived at the hotel shortly thereafter. When I arrived, I saw several fire trucks parked near the hotel. Then I ran inside, and the first floor was covered in about 5-6 inches of water. All the people who were sleeping on the first floor, including the Japanese, Koreans and other people who came from other states were in the lobby. The firefighters were sweating as they pushed out the water from the hallway floor with wide and large shovels. After hearing the story of how it happened, I didn't know what to say because this situation was so unbelievable.

Later, we found out that a fire sprinkler unexpectedly went off, causing one of the Japanese people's rooms to be flooded.

Fed Up with My Eternal Enemy

I was so shocked that I was speechless, and I didn't know what to do. But I knew right away it was the same spiritual attack against the Japanese people as last year. I was so angry and fed up with the attacks. "You dirty Satan!" was the first word that came out of my mouth. "I command you in Jesus' name to immediately let go of the Japanese people who came desiring the presence of God. I bind every spirit that's trying to come against our conference, in Jesus' name. I command you in Jesus' name to let go of God's people now and go! Stop your demonic plans now! In Jesus' name, I command the principalities and powers of darkness to leave!"

I continued with my spiritual warfare with a loud voice and kept praying to bind the enemy (Matthew 18:18). Thankfully, all of the conference attendees who were murmuring and saying, "Amen, Amen," then they began to agree with my declaration and joined me with their heavenly language and in spiritual warfare.

After praying, and without complaining or saying any negative words, all of the Japanese conferees rolled up their sleeves and pants, and with bare feet, they borrowed the huge shovel from the firefighters and helped push out the water. It was absolutely a beautiful scene. I didn't know if I should cry or laugh, as I joined them.

The hotel manager didn't know how to react. With teary eyes she said, "How can this possibly happen?" The conference was growing every year so, we always reserved the same hotel a year in advance. The hotel manager was overwhelmed with this terrible situation, and she did not know what to do. Unfortunately, the beds were drenched in water, and the floor was all wet, so we had to transfer most of the Japanese people to a neighboring hotel at three o'clock in the morning.

Cold Atmosphere

The news about the flood incident in the hotel quickly spread to those on the second floor who slept without awareness of what had happened. The intercessory meeting started at 9 a.m., but since the Japanese people were unable to sleep the night before, the atmosphere was cold and heavy. As the meeting started, the worship minister praised in faith against the heaviness and coldness in the atmosphere, and captured our hearts with beautiful spiritual songs that ignited our hearts. Our faithful Holy Spirit who knows our needs very well began to work fast. He was showing us what we needed and what we needed to do.

Mature Intercessor's Ministry

Most of the people who attended the Intercessory Prayer Conference were those who regularly came every year. They were the ones who learned how to pray for spiritual breakthroughs with the help of the Holy Spirit. Praise the Lord that those who were in the intercessory prayer meeting did not take long to realize that it was the enemy's attack to distract the people from receiving the spiritual breakthroughs. Without any hesitation, the intercessors approached the Japanese people. Some of them, despite the language barrier, started travailing prayer and interceded with tears for their guests. Others embraced the Japanese people tightly and interceded for their spiritual breakthrough. Without a doubt, they realized that this love and comfort was from Jesus and the Japanese people were extremely touched. At the same time, their spiritual breakthrough began.

Undeniable Presence of the Lord

That afternoon, the Holy Spirit dominated the service. All conferees freely praised the Lord with one heart and danced together joyfully like little children. More than ever before, the fiery worship and praise led them to experience freedom from the Devil's bondage. Thankfully, through the intercessors' sincere prayers, the Japanese people experienced greater spiritual breakthrough and the powerful work of the Holy Spirit. In the years that followed, the Japanese people continued to attend the conference, and we interceded for the revival of Japan. Amazingly, their excitement to come back to Sunshine Ministries Conference has grown every year.

True Freedom in Jesus

Every year the Japanese people returned to the conference, they showed great progress in their spiritual maturity. When I saw that they were experiencing true freedom in Christ, and the yokes that oppressed them were broken off, I was confident that this was the work of God and His ability, thus I give all the glory to the Lord.

I am always extremely proud of the Japanese intercessors. Seeing themselves change each time they enter and leave America, they are always willing to pay a high price to come to learn spiritual warfare every year. Absolutely, this is God's grace and power. I also thank God for every opportunity I've had to travel to Japan, including 75 trips, until Covid-19, in 2020. I pray that God will give me many more years to travel and see Japan's revival.

CHAPTER 13

THE POWER AND BLESSING
OF INTERCESSORY PRAYER

The Power and Blessing of Intercessory Prayer

Intercessors experience happiness in life when they see their prayers answered, hear the voice of God, and receive power and blessings from being united with Him. God resolves our problems when we look beyond ourselves and above our circumstances and pray for others. As we continue to intercede, the power and blessings will eventually follow. Once we realize this truth, we will not grow tired or feel the task is too great when we are interceding. If we pray according to the guidance of the Holy Spirit, we will receive an overflowing of God's blessing.

Even now, I practice every day to posture my heart as an intercessor and to be sensitive to the leading of the Holy Spirit. The more I intercede for others, the more God's special favor and blessing overflows to me. The anointing of the Holy Spirit manifests to me stronger day by day so that I can do the ministry of expanding the Kingdom of God. And wherever I travel throughout the world, God's healing and miraculous works continue to take place.

Because We Don't Intercede

Today's churches are unlike the early churches in demonstration of prayer and power because too many believers are ruled by the lust of the flesh, the lust of the eyes, and the pride of life. And they are constantly oppressed by the Devil because their faith is self-centered, egoistical, and they don't intercede for others. The church is weak because believers are only praying for their own problems.

These religious people are not respected by those around them and often hurt others. They only think about themselves and ask others to pray for them all the time. Thus, it's hard to see progress in their Christian life and they are stagnant in their faith. They are unaware that we accumulate spiritual garbage when we don't intercede and consequently are unable to do God's work. Intercessory prayer is an essential prayer because it enables us to continuously do God's work and helps us to grow spiritually.

The Power and Blessings of Intercessors
1. Happiness of Life

A loving person is a happy person. An interceding person is also a happy person. A loving person is a person who thinks about others first. When someone's hurt or is in pain, or an emergency arises and an answer is needed, intercessors are the first to pray. Compared to someone who focuses on their own problems and prays only for themselves, those who pray for others will live a life full of joy and receive abundant blessings in everything they do.

In order to receive God's blessing, we must do as He wants us to do. Because many people don't realize this simple truth, they go about here and there looking for blessings. For example, it becomes a blessing when finances follow me, but it is painstaking when I try to chase after them. When we entrust our entire live to God through prayer, we receive God's peace and joy of overflowing blessings. This is a fundamental principle in God's way of dealing with us. However, we will become exhausted when we go after the blessings with our own efforts.

2. Answer to Prayer

I have countless testimonies of answers to intercessory prayer that I can't begin to list them all here. It's hard to put it in numbers how many times God led me to pray and how soon He answered my prayers. The answers to our prayers are God's power and blessing.

3. Being One with God

We become one with God through prayer and enter His realm. Then, we can have all that He has. The people in this world may see us as poor and uneducated, but when we enter God's presence, we become one with Him and all that belongs to Him becomes ours, and we can say that, "I am strong and rich." And the blessing is that we can share what we receive with others.

My existence is to solely be the messenger who relay's God's healing and God's power through intercessory prayer.

Intercessors are never weak but instead are unfailingly strong. It is because we have a special privilege of being united with God.

AFTERWORD

Intercessory Prayer Is Not a Special Gift

In finishing this book, I want to say that it doesn't require that you have a special gift to do intercessory prayer. When we fix our eyes on the Lord and look beyond our own problems and pray for others, that is intercessory prayer. Just like there are steps of growth, our prayer life starts with praying for ourselves, but later we must develop the level of maturity of praying for others. Furthermore, we get to experience the place of the Holy of Holies, where we solely praise, worship, and love God, and this makes it easier for us to enter the His presence. We must progress to this level. There is a vital difference when we look at someone and think, *Poor thing,* versus when we pray with God's heart for that person.

We will overflow with blessings and the power of God when we pray for others with God's heart as an intercessor. Therefore, we must always examine ourselves to see if there's any root of bitterness that's hindering our prayers, and if God shows us our unrighteousness, any actions of wrongdoings, and that root of bitterness, we must quickly confess our sins, repent, and fast for our wounds to be healed. In order for us to be effective intercessors, we must resolve the wounds within us; only then can we devote ourselves to others and sacrificially intercede for them. If there are many wounds and problems within me, whenever I come before God to pray, I won't have time to intercede for others because I'm too occupied with praying for my problems. Though we may do this unconsciously, our biggest problem is that we think that our thoughts are wiser than God's and consequently we don't obey His word.

Experiencing the Holy Spirit and Spiritual Breakthrough

The reason why so many intercessors come to the Sunshine International Ministries Intercessory Prayer Conference is because they receive the fire of the Holy Spirit and His overflowing grace, and experience spiritual breakthrough and change. That is the reward God pours out upon the intercessors. It is not something that I can do or give. Without a doubt, it is the work of the Holy Spirit and the grace of God.

The Bible tells us that when two or three are gathered, the Spirit of God is in their midst (Matthew 18:20). When believers humbly lay down their egos and gaze upon the Lord, then the work of the Holy Spirit will manifest whenever and wherever we are.

What makes our conference a little different from others, I would say, is the frequent times of intercession throughout the conference. During intercessory prayer time, one of my disciples and a psalmist begins to worship with prophetic new songs, led by the Holy Spirit, with the heavenly voice that God has given her and guides people to examine themselves. The conference is centered around the people first confessing their sins before the Lord, receiving forgiveness, and experiencing spiritual breakthroughs. Then everyone can unite together and earnestly and passionately intercede for their families, churches, and nations. Because from hour to hour they encounter the deeper presence of the Lord and spiritual breakthroughs, they are willing to attend by paying a high price as they fast and intercede. God sees their sacrifice and devotion, and surely, He greatly blesses them.

Abundant Joyful Life

Do you want to be greatly used by God as an intercessor? Do you want to glorify Him? Look around your surroundings to see who is in need. Rather than praying for your problems, try praying for other people's problems. And not only do you pray, but you should also show your concern in action. Just like how the faith of four friends led to the healing of the paralyzed man, our faith will also bring life to our neighbors and raise up the church (Luke 5:18-25). Our intercessory prayer life creates a truly happy life. An intercessor whom God delights in is one who moves beyond their limitations, circumstances, and their own problems. Humility is putting others first and God takes pleasure in that kind of humility.

I highly urge you to become an intercessory prayer warrior who pleases God. You will then live a life that is joyful and fruitful, and one that you cannot live without prayer.

God bless you and all that you do for His kingdom!

Dr. Sun Fannin